7350

"Ladies and gentlemen,

MR. HARRY
'RED'
FOSTER"

Dedicated to
my wife Janet who worked while I played
and to H. Jane and Andrew at NC
for invaluable editorial assistance.

"Ladies and gentlemen,

Mr. Harry 'Red' Foster"

Paul E. Lewis

NC PRESS LIMITED
Toronto, 1004

Canadian Cataloguing Publication Data

Lewis, Paul E.
   Ladies and Gentlemen - Mr. Harry "Red" Foster

Includes bibliographic references and index.
ISBN 1-55021-078-5

1. Foster, Harry Edward, 1905-1985. 2. Advertising - Ontario - Biography.
3. Foster Advertising Limited. 4. Radio broadcasters - Canada - Biography.
5. Canadian Special Olympics Inc. I. Title.

HF5810.F67L4 1994 659.1'092 C94-932225-3

We would like to thank the Ontario Arts Council, the Ontario Publishing Centre, the Ontario Ministry of Culture, Tourism and Recreation, the Ontario Development Corporation, the Canada Council, and the Government of Canada, Department of Communications, for their assistance in the production of this book.

New Canada Publications, a division of NC Press Limited,
Box 452, Station A, Toronto, Ontario, Canada, M5W 1H8.

Printed and bound in Canada.

Contents

Preface

I began this project innocently enough, five summers ago with a serendipitous search through a mass of unorganized paper and memorabilia that constituted the archives at Ridley College in St. Catharines. Buried in one box were a few old school report cards and one of those was Harry E. Foster's from 1924. His report revealed an academic disaster. Farther away, in the corner of one of the school's playing fields sits a memorial cairn, placed there in 1986 to honour Harry as one of Ridley's illustrious sons. Curiosity filled the next few summers with further research and this led to a sabbatical year from the school to bring Harry's exciting life story to light. There have been no regrets.

Harry Foster was a complex individual. He cultivated a wide circle of friends and acquaintances on many different social levels. Those who knew him were inclined to be aware of one or sometimes two of his many dimensions — as school mate, as sportsman, as churchman, as business executive, as organizational dynamo, as family friend or as friend of the movement for the mentally handicapped. Bringing all of the dimensions of Harry's multi-faceted career between two covers has been a real challenge. Harry did not write much on a personal level himself but relied heavily upon competent secretaries and on the telephone (and sometimes two of these at once). This led to my reliance on an extensive interviewing process that was thoroughly enjoyable and I am greatly indebted to the many people who were kind enough to share their reminiscences of life with Harry. That I have missed a few is inevitable. In particular, I am especially grateful to Ms Carol Davis-Kerr in the Foster Foundation for simply being helpful, and to two long-standing former Foster Advertising employees, Mr. Bill Orrett and Mr. Bill Whitehead who were so generous with their time.

The research process was also assisted by Harry's own propensity to save things. To claim that Harry had a sense of history is perhaps saying too much. It would be more appropriate, I think, to suggest that Harry had a sense of occasion. This was a characteristic he got from his mother who did keep a book of newspaper scraps which recorded many of Harry's broadcasting appearances in the 1930's. These scraps made the job of finding the others much easier. Also in the 1930's and through into the 1960's, one of Harry's best friends was the brilliant sports columnist of the *Toronto Telegram*, the late Ted Reeve. Reeve kept his readership abreast of many of Harry's activities and once one gets used to reading between Reeve's lines, his columns and comments proved incredibly helpful. In his later career, Harry himself collected an enormous quantity of film, tape recordings and photographs which marked the various occasions in his life, and much of this material has survived the ravages of time.

In 1978, Harry decided to donate to the Public Archives of Canada his remarkably complete collection of radio material which sprang from his own studios in the 1940's. This collection, dating from the Golden Age of Radio consists of nearly 2000 sound recordings and 18 boxes of original scripts. That the material was saved at all from the hazards of fire, flood and housecleaning over the years is a minor miracle. Historians now have access to what some of early Canadian radio was like from the perspective of a private broadcaster. In 1993, arrangements were made by the Foster Foundation for the depositing of the rest of Harry's papers, recordings, photographs and films with our national archives. Preparing that collection for posterity is now underway. Sadly, the records from Harry E. Foster Advertising Limited have not survived.

Harry moved from Toronto to Oakville in 1950 and took up residence in a modest home that was once the Gate House to the old Ennisclare Estate. His wife Jimmie, now almost 90 years of age, still resides there in comfort. The only obvious luxury is a small swimming pool deep in the trees at the back of the grassy property. Harry could easily have afforded a more palatial dwelling but, perhaps reflecting his own middle class upbringing, such things were neither needed by him nor of interest. Stories abound of Harry's invitations to lunch to colleagues in Toronto and leaving them with the bill, or his idea of lunch at the Granite Club ending up in the locker room with a sandwich and a can of pop. These were indications of a certain frugality but, more importantly, of a mind that was usually racing ahead to more important things. He did own a northern camp in Quebec, twenty minutes by float plane out of North Bay. Two or three times a year, he would use it to entertain clients and/or friends. What he most enjoyed there was the time the camp gave him to paddle off and be alone with his own thoughts, regrouping as it were for the weeks of hectic activity that always lay ahead of him.

Piecing Harry's story together has been a tremendously satisfying experience for me and I regard the many new friends I have made during the process as a lasting bonus. That the work was finished in 1994, the year that marks the 25th anniversary of the founding of the Canadian Special Olympics, and the beginning and the end of Foster Advertising (1934-1994) is entirely coincidental. If the readers of Harry's generation smile in fond remembrance or if the more youthful readers of the 1990's are inspired in any way by what Harry Foster accomplished, then I will consider my endeavour as a success.

Paul E. Lewis

Introduction

One afternoon in the late 1930's, a few days before Christmas, a youthful crowd could be seen funnelling its way into Maple Leaf Gardens in Toronto. Lined up all the way around the building were hundreds of cheerful chattering children; streetcars and buses were delivering further hordes by the minute. No pied piper was in sight, but some sort of magnet was evidently at work. At one side entrance, large shiny automobiles were lined up and crippled children were being lifted from them by athletic looking gentlemen. All of these excited looking children were members of Harry "Red" Foster's Crown Brand Sports Club arriving for the spectacular Christmas Ice Carnival. No admission charges were being taken, but each youngster could be seen proudly wearing the only requirement of the day, a numbered Crown Brand Sports Club button.

The long anticipated annual show for Club members was really one gigantic promotion for Corn Syrup sponsored by the Canada Starch Company. Harry himself was the organizer and master of ceremonies for these three hour extravaganzas, which were blends of circus and variety club acts on ice. Since parents were not invited, Harry had to demonstrate some remarkable child psychology in maintaining control of his 15,000 exuberant fans. His method was to give the throng hearty doses of noise, top flight action drawn primarily from the world of sports, and short doses of homely virtue and good cheer. In between the various events, Harry would have the children give three cheers for Santa Claus, three cheers for Toronto or three cheers for Canada to let off steam, first the boys, then the girls and then the wolf cubs and so on. He would have them sing "Hail, Hail, The Gang's All Here" and then profess a little disappointment in the volume and have them do it all again. He had them singing and clapping or remaining silent exactly on cue. He loved having fun with children. This was their day. In Harry, the kids in turn saw a noisy, jovial and genuine friend.

This event, coming somewhere near the middle of his career, illustrates many of the aspects of Harry Foster's character, his method of operation, and the answer to why his career was so successful. He was motivated from his earliest days to live life to the fullest and always to have fun doing it. Harry liked being the centre of attention, he liked success and he liked to make money. Sometimes he got carried away with his own enthusiasm and the intensity of his ideas, and some people would see him as aggressive because of this. Harry had an uncanny knack of seeing opportunities, both in business and in society, and of pursuing them with dogged determination. He was a true salesman who maintained the highest of personal standards

An advertisement for Harry Foster's Crown Brand Sports Club showing the membership button in the top left corner.

and who also understood the importance of both social conscience and social responsibility. His Christmas Ice Carnivals, for instance, were designed to give children a free and wholesome good time. Not only could he regularly pack Maple Leaf Gardens with 15,000 eager youngsters, but he could also talk dozens of sports celebrities and local dignitaries into sharing the limelight with him for a good cause. Harry was a promoter who loved recognition although some people would interpret this as vanity. When thwarted with adversity or personal tragedy, he had the gift of landing back on two feet and pressing on. Above all other things that motivated him, however, Harry Foster had a sincere love for all people both great and small. He cultivated a passion for Canada and demonstrated throughout his life a special brand of affection for children.

These motivating factors combined with the characteristics which defined his personality, fashioned a career which filled Harry's life with numerous crowning moments well beyond what most people ever experience. He played on a dozen championship sports teams before he was twenty. He could claim to be an international champion racing-boat driver. He helped win a Grey Cup Championship in football when he was twenty-five. He pioneered a series of firsts in the early days of radio broadcasting and was the Master of Ceremonies for a segment of the Royal Visit to Toronto in 1939. Harry was the guardian for the Dionne Quintuplets when he escorted them to Superior, Wisconsin to launch five Victory Ships during the Second World War. In 1966, he won the Gold Medal from the Association of Canadian Advertisers as Advertising Man of the Year and in 1969 the Medal of Service of the Order of Canada. He accepted both the Royal Bank and the B'Nai Brith Awards for humanitarian service toward the end of his career and, one year before his death in 1985, Harry Foster was inducted as a builder into Canada's Sports Hall of Fame.

In 1904, a year before Harry Foster was born, Sir Wilfrid Laurier uttered one of the great and long remembered one liners of Canadian history when he said that "the 20th century shall be the century of Canada." What the Prime Minister meant was that Canada would continue to develop economically on the strength of an enormous resource base; she would take her rightful place among the nations of the world, and would establish an identity of her own as a people and as a nation. Laurier's prophecy was fulfilled in many ways, but it could not have been realized without the efforts of countless ordinary citizens who both shared the dream and also worked out its details in the course of their lives. These include the builders, the farmers, the soldiers, the educators and the captains of industry, each of whom in his or her own way made contributions to our national welfare. One of these contributors was Harry E. Foster of Toronto. As sportsman, business entrepreneur, advocate of free enterprise and philanthropist, his career rode the crest of that wave of development which Canada has experienced so dramatically in this century.

In many ways, Harry "Red" Foster lived a double life. He built a remarkably successful advertising business, made a great deal of money and enjoyed the good life. At the same time he cultivated a genuine and conscious interest in making life better for others. He blended together both aspects of this double life, although he was probably quite unaware that he was doing so. His actions and his deeds were simply what came naturally to him. As his business career took on a life of its own, he directed his efforts into doing a tremendous amount of good and into trying to make Canada a better place. He channelled his boundless energy and resources into improving the condition of a specific group of unfortunate citizens, the mentally disabled. A strong sense of purpose seemed to mark everything he did and the accomplishments themselves were the result of a combination both of nature, what his personality dictated, and of nurture, what his life experiences taught him. That fortunate combination resulted in the remarkable story of a very special Canadian.

Chapter One
4 Oaklands Avenue

Harry Foster's birth in 1905 was quite unspectacular, except of course in the eyes of his parents, Daniel and Helen Foster, of 4 Oaklands Avenue in Toronto. Their first born son was a welcomed and certainly expected addition to the family tree. The roots of the Foster tree went back to St. Mary's, Ontario, where grandfather John Foster, of second generation Irish stock, had owned a flourishing dry goods business. He left St. Mary's in the mid 1880's with his wife Elizabeth and their three children, Lily, Edward and Daniel, and re-established himself in a similar wholesaling business in Toronto. The intention undoubtedly was that the new enterprise would provide a base that at least one of the boys could take over, and be a cushion for his own retirement years as well. He must have been reasonably successful because, just after the turn of the century, the whole

Harry's boyhood home at 4 Oaklands Avenue in Toronto.

family settled in a new house on Oaklands Avenue. It was located in the Cottingham district just opening up in what was then the northern fringe of the city. It was a modest brick duplex with a back yard surrounded by a high board fence. These fences, behind so many houses of that area, were a characteristic architectural feature of the era. Oaklands would always be the home base of the Foster clan even after Lily and Edward had moved on to their own houses. Harry's family was always a close knit one and there were bonds of affection among all members which Harry would carry with him throughout his life. Family gatherings on Oaklands Avenue were frequent and there was a strong feeling among all Fosters of the need to look after one another. An old age home for Harry's grandparents, for instance, would have been out of the question, even if there had been such things at the time. Both would die at home, John in 1916, and Elizabeth in 1919.

The two sons, Edward and Daniel, wasted little time in establishing themselves after completing their high school education. Edward continued the family wholesale business tradition begun by his father. He would eventually become an importer and exporter, buying and selling dry goods, textiles and draperies to firms which included Eaton's and Simpsons. His offices were in downtown Toronto until the early 1930's when he moved to Montreal. Daniel, Harry's father, began his business career with grandfather Foster as well. When John Foster retired, however, Daniel left Edward to carry on alone and joined the H.S. Howland & Sons wholesale hardware business. He started literally at the bottom, but hard work and an instinct for sales saw him advance from clerk to traveller to buyer

Harry as a boy at the family cottage on Wilcox Lake, 1909.

and, after only fifteen years, to become the manager of the whole Toronto operation.

What Harry Foster was born into in 1905 was a solid, hard working, middle class, business oriented family. There was sufficient money for some worldly goods but few reported luxuries. Harry was always a well-dressed child. Photographs of the family show quite modest means and a concern for their public image. At home, there was enough coal for the winter, electric lights and running water, which at the time were the symbols of a certain degree of affluence. By the time of the First World War there was a car in the garage, a small cottage on Wilcox Lake north of Toronto, and sufficient security to consider sending Harry to a private school. The influences on young Harry centered on family ties and the world of business enterprise. Two of his role models, his uncle and his father, taught that honest and fair dealings with customers coupled with hard work brought visible results.

However important the world of work was in giving the family its stability, it was never seen as an all consuming passion. Work was merely a way of making the other things of life possible. Most important among the other things in the Foster family was a keen interest in sports. Encouragement in this area came mostly from Harry's father, an avid rugby player in his youth and a fan of many sports in his later life. In Daniel's early Toronto days he had been the quarterback for the old Excelsiors Rugby Club, and just after the turn of the century he became a well known figure in bicycling circles, once winning the Dunlop Time Prize, given for a bicycle race along Kingston Road. He eventually became the president of the prestigious Century Cycling Club. To become a member of this club, it was necessary to ride one hundred miles in a single day. The Foster family took great pride in the fact that Harry's Aunt Lily had done just that in the year 1891 to become only the second female in Canada to have accomplished that feat. She had gone from Toronto to Newcastle and back on a wooden-rimmed hand-braked bicycle, returning fourteen hours later covered with dust and personal honour.

While interest in and support for sports was part of the Foster family tradition, the Cottingham Square area of Toronto where they lived was also a powerful influence in Harry Foster's early school days. Harry entered Cottingham Public School in 1911 and would advance steadily through it. It was known at the time to be in a particularly tough neck of the woods where the rough and tumble of the school yard was certainly as much of a learning situation as the class-

Cottingham Public School in Toronto.

room. One schoolmate recalls that Harry Foster was always a leader in the yard. He fought his share of battles but never gave the impression that he was too busy to be a friend to anybody. His schoolmate's strongest memory was a winter school yard game where one boy would stand against the wall while others would fire chunks of ice hopefully just over his head. Harry always took his turn against the wall.

The whole Cottingham area of Toronto was a hotbed of sporting activities all year long; this was due in some measure to the shadow cast by the sporting lives of the great Conacher family who lived a short distance away on Davenport Road. A strong and lasting friendship between Charlie Conacher and Harry Foster dates from their early school days and both boys undoubtedly idolized Charlie's brother Lionel, whose exploits on the sports fields were becoming legendary. Ted Reeve, sports writer for *The Toronto Evening Telegram*, once wrote that "every kid in Cottingham Square or Jesse Ketchum Park [the Conacher base nearby] played lacrosse, rugby and hockey and you had to fight or move." After school, weekends and holidays were consumed with sand-lot baseball, road and ice hockey and lacrosse. The famous Maitlands Lacrosse Club used

Cottingham Square as its home base and Harry must have watched many games there as he was developing into a proficient player in his own right.

It seemed like the most natural thing in the world for young adolescents like Harry to be active participants in the seasonal round of solid team sports. There was such a large group of like-minded boys in Harry's neighbourhood that fielding a pick-up team almost any time was taken as a matter of course. Winter hockey blended into springtime baseball which blended into summer lacrosse and then autumn rugby. Harry was a natural athlete and he played the games with an avid passion that is remembered by all who knew him. Another of his schoolmates recalls a popular Foster pastime of the summer in Cottingham Square. With one or two other boys, Harry would kick a rugby ball back and forth for hours on end and practice running flying tackles until darkness set in. What emerged in his early boyhood was a passion for sports, and particularly rugby, an excellent natural ability, a willingness to take the bumps and knocks of team games, and a fierce competitive spirit. Harry played by the rules to win but even more, played for the fun and camaraderie that the games offered.

Cottingham Square, now called Conacher Park, across the street from Cottingham Public School.

The interest in sports, the supportive family and the large circle of sporting friends were strong influences on Harry's growing-up years. Yet there was another influence which was even stronger, one whose impact would be even more powerful and much longer lasting, than any of the others. In 1911, during Harry's first year at Cottingham School, a baby brother, John Orr Foster, was added to the family circle. Soon after the boy's birth, his parents noticed a problem with his eyesight and specialists undertook delicate surgery. Sadly, and after various operations over two years, they managed to save only one eye. In addition to this, even before his second birthday, the Fosters became aware that the boy's development was clearly lagging behind that of normal infants. Visits to doctors and specialists confirmed the diagnosis. Jackie, as he was known in the family, was mentally retarded.[1]

The full realization of the implications that this situation created for the family came slowly. Known now as Down's Syndrome, it meant the need for virtually full time care for the boy. What is now known about mental disability, which still strikes about three in every one hundred children, was not known in the early 20th century. There was, then, a horror and a grief which could only be shared by the parents themselves. Society attached a sense of shame to the condition and there was certainly no available treatment. Keeping these afflicted children out of sight was the accepted practice. When Jackie was six years old, the Fosters tried sending him to kindergarten but, within a couple of days, Helen Foster was told to keep the boy at home.

What impact Jackie's existence had on Harry in the early years is speculative. From evidence later in his life, we can surmise that Harry always accepted Jackie completely, as an equal member of the family. Jackie responded to love and affection and there was plenty of that in the Foster home. Whether Harry's energy and reported scrap-

A redrawing of a sketch which accompanied the article "The Lady on My Street" *by Harry E. (Red) Foster by Jakubowski,* The Toronto Telegram, *November 20, 1959.*

piness in the school yard came from his defence of his little brother or whether somehow he tried to live his own and his brother's life at the same time will never really be known. The fact that Harry developed a bubbly and enthusiastic

---

[1] The term "mentally retarded" is historically accurate. The terms "people with developmental handicaps," "mentally handicapped," and "mentally disabled" are the preferred current usage.

personality with an almost perpetual sense of humour is all the more remarkable in the light of the potential for family gloom. As Harry often said later when referring to how his mother in particular coped with the burden, "There was no crepe on our door." In any event, by Jackie's eighth birthday, he had become totally blind and thus totally dependent on the care of his family members. The idea of putting Jackie in an institution was never considered; the Fosters always looked after their own.

Aside from Jackie's disability, something that clearly had a long term and powerful impact on Harry was watching how his mother coped with the problem. For her, there was time only for caring and none for brooding. Every single day, after getting Harry off to school and father off to work, and looking after all of Jackie's basic needs, she would walk courageously around the block with him, arm in arm, past the curious stares and, sometimes, the unthinking laughter of children. This daily exercise went on for thirty years for Jackie and for his family, and especially for his mother. There can be little doubt that Harry's sensitivity to the needs of the handicapped dates from these early years at home.

Caring for Jackie's needs, which was a family responsibility, and Daniel's efforts in the wholesale hardware business would suggest that Harry's early childhood was characterized by regular routines. Remaining fragments of information suggest that summertime was always the most pleasant time of year for the Fosters when the routines changed. Father almost always took holidays then and they would go north to Wilcox Lake for a few weeks of relaxation and a break in the routine for Helen and Jackie. As well, Harry often spent a week or two at the YMCA's Camp Pinecrest in Muskoka where he managed to win the all round athletic championship at least twice. It was there too that he developed a love for fishing and for the wilderness which never left him. Later in his life, he would escape periodically to the tranquillity of his own wilderness camp in northern Quebec. Stuck in Harry's memory of his youth, was also an occasional trip with his father across the

Cottingham Public School's 1919 championship winning hockey team. Harry is in the centre row, second from the left.

Toronto Bay to Toronto Island to see a lacrosse game and to visit the amusement centre which operated there in the summertime. Harry was never particularly interested in spectator sports, however. Participation was far more interesting and his base, Cottingham Square, was where he was happiest.

How the Foster family coped with the problems everyone faced during the years of the First World War is not known. Daniel Foster was hard at work, Helen Foster had her hands full with Jackie's care and Harry went through the daily routines at Cottingham Public School. Harry did sell newspapers at Birch and Yonge streets to earn spending money during the later war years and he was also a part-time red cap at the North Toronto CPR station nearby. This latter experience gave him his only exposure to the Great War as he witnessed many troop trains as they returned to Toronto from the east. At 12 and 13 years of age, Harry was too young to understand all the complexities of a war based society; however, the fact that Toronto's wartime mayor, Tommy Church, used to come to the station to greet these trains at all hours of the day or night was a vivid childhood memory that Harry would recall many times later in his life. Mayor Church may have been politically motivated, but Harry interpreted his train station visits as simply an indication of how Toronto's fighting men should be treated. A grateful city should honour those who had sacrificed themselves in the cause of freedom.

The year 1919 marked the death of Harry's grandmother Elizabeth and the signing of the Peace Settlement after the Great War. It was also Harry's last year at Cottingham School. The highlights of that final year for the school were the city Public School Soccer Championship in the fall and the Senior Public School Minor Hockey League Championship in the winter. The fact that Harry was captain and centre man of both of these teams attests to his abilities as a player and to his qualities as a team leader, qualities which were recognized by his peers and teachers alike. The young sportsman advanced from Cottingham Public School to Davenport High School in the fall of 1920, and there he played on every available junior soccer, hockey, and football team. Harry played a key role in helping Davenport to win the Toronto Junior High School Hockey Championship in 1921. He also played outside his school in the Toronto Hockey League with the Aura Lee Junior Team. It is hard to imagine the youngster Harry Foster with much spare time on his hands as he continued his part-time red cap job at the CPR station and also pursued his enthusiastic involvement in school and neighbourhood sports activities. Packing each day with a full schedule was a Harry Foster characteristic which had its roots in childhood.

Early in 1922, the Fosters began to realize that the sporting life which was consuming young Harry was inadequate in itself. Grades 9 and 10 at Davenport High School had been a success in the sporting sense but had not gone that well academically. Harry had certainly passed from grade to grade but he showed little interest in academic matters. Looking further into the future, both parents were beginning to believe that an element of academic discipline might redirect his sports-loving spirit into more promising channels. Furthermore, the care of brother Jackie, now eleven years old, was consuming virtually all of the waking hours of the day for his mother. While Harry never lacked attention, the whole family understood that Jackie deserved a degree of priority. A different school for Harry in a different environment might be the answer to a number of concerns, so Daniel Foster consequently made the decision to enrol Harry at Ridley College in St. Catharines beginning in September. This was a decision which meant a financial sacrifice for the family, but it would mark a major turning point in Harry's life.

Chapter Two
School Days

While the largest of boys' boarding schools in Canada had always had a reputation for both academic excellence and rigid discipline, Ridley College was also known for its dedication to competitive sports. Whether father Foster realized it at the time, Harry would continue his active involvement in sports of all kinds. Chiefly responsible for Ridley's fine reputation in this regard was its second Headmaster, Dr. Harry J. Griffith. Griffith had previously taught at the University of Toronto, and in addition was the coach of the Varsity rugby-football team. This team, under his direction, had earned the first Dominion Grey Cup titles in 1909, 1910 and 1911.

Football was Griffith's passion in the autumn, with hockey in the winter and cricket in the spring rounding out

Ridley College in the 1920's. Harry Foster was a student at Ridley in 1923 when the new chapel opened as a memorial to Ridley alumni killed in the First World War.

the school year. In football, "The Griff," as he was affectionately known, was always active teaching the basics, encouraging his boys to develop the skills and to learn the plays which would win games. He had in fact written most of the rule book for Canadian football which added to his aura as an authority. More importantly, however, was the

Harry Foster in grade 12 at Ridley College, 1923.

fact that Griffith taught the boys the value of sport for its own sake, the strength of teamwork and the importance of sportsmanship. They would be gentlemen at all times. His motto was, "If you win, say nothing; if you lose, say less." These were lessons his players learned and remembered long after the games were over. It was under this sort of direction that young Harry built his skills based on an already keen competitive spirit.

In Red's first term at Ridley, he not only played on the First Football Team, but also made a strong contribution in a series of victories that led the school to the championship in the Independent School League. Each member of the team was presented with a tiny silver football for his efforts, although the thrill of chalking up another championship under Coach Griffith was considered reward enough. Foster was noted in the school yearbook's football analysis for 1922 as, "a sure catch, a good kick, a very fast and tricky runner. Combined well with the other backs and was indefatigable at all times." This note could have been written almost any time over the next eight years.

Harry seems to have fitted himself into the daily routines of private school with ease. He was remembered as being popular with his friends and noted for his kindness to others in his class although the recollections of the older boys suggest that he was a bit of a show-off. This observation is typical of the feeling that many senior students seem to have when confronted with any sort of junior overconfidence. One consistent memory among those who knew him then, however, was that Red got along well with everyone. A rare letter home (written in schoolboy poetry) illustrates a little of the life at boarding school and shows Foster as generous and gregarious but also with an eye for minor mischief. It reads:

Dear Mother,

I received your box, the chicken and the cake. Last night our dorm all had a feed, and everything was jake.

A master almost caught us though I don't think he'll do much, except perhaps just lick us, and then we'd be in dutch.

There's nothing happening here just now, except the same old things; soccer, gym and basketball or else the boxing ring.

Jim and I went to the store, and of course it's out of bounds, because it's only on half-holidays we're allowed outside the grounds.

As we were on our way alas! two masters came in view.

Ridley College Hockey Team, 1923. Dr. Harry Griffith sits in the front row, left. Harry Foster is in the back row behind him.

Every place I go it seems I meet not less than two.

I don't think that they saw me, though I got an awful fright. But just the same if they got my name, I'll surely know tonight.

When you have time, please write.

Your loving son, H.[E.]F.

If he and his friend had been caught "out of bounds" they would have been punished, perhaps with the cane, but no record or later memory remains to indicate any consequences from this particular case.

The highlight during the course of the first year for all boys new to the school was the annual New Boy Concert. This was a traditional exercise engineered by the seniors to test the mettle of the newcomers and to provide themselves with entertainment. Harry Foster's contribution on this occasion was in a quartet session of jokes and songs, which is on record as a smashing success. Typical of the reaction

The Ridley College Choir, June, 1924. Harry Foster is in the back row, fifth from the left.

to amateur school performances to this day, some students thought that the concert was no good and some that it was the best ever; but everyone agreed that the Foster numbers were among the outstanding items.

He evidently displayed a certain stage presence or at least a certain confident ease on the stage which, unknown at the time of course, would be of enormous importance later in his life. Whether he uncovered these talents at Ridley or whether the talent simply emerged with the opportunities that the school provided is uncertain. Harry was certainly no shrinking violet during the course of his high school career. It is not surprising that during one of the breaks from school, Harry and two of his Toronto friends organized a whole amateur show one evening at The Bloor Street Theatre. This was a 1923 version of a modern "Yuk-Yuks" performance in the days when live stage shows were a popular form of entertainment. The details of the program have not survived, but the fact that Harry was doing this sort of thing when he was only eighteen years old underlines his natural leadership talent, his fondness for being front and centre, and his ability to create a good time.

Maintaining contact with his Toronto friends was a normal feature of Harry's private school days. Ridley was never seen as some far away institution that would shut a boy off from familiar surroundings. The prep schools in fact were always in contact, especially with their athletic contests, which were seen as much as social occasions as sporting events. In the Ridley games against Upper Canada College in particular, Harry's father was almost always in attendance. He always brought Jackie, and the pair became a familiar sight on the sidelines. While Jackie could not see the action, he is reported to have enjoyed the cheering. This sort of fatherly attention is perhaps to be expected, but more interesting and indicative of Harry's own disposition, was the fact that both father and disabled brother were included in the post-game social hours. Harry had no problem in introducing Jackie to his own friends and including him in the fun. During those social hours, Harry and his father always conferred about Harry's playing efforts. Daniel's interest and experience in sports made Harry an eager listener. There is no doubt that the bonds between father and son were strengthened during Harry's Ridley years.

Ridley College Rugby Football Team, 1923. Harry Foster is eighth from the left in the semi-circle.

Harry's athletic ability, especially in football, must have been a treat for any father to watch. His skating talent was also good enough to watch. It earned him a regular spot on the First Hockey Team in his first year; unfortunately the team as a whole was not strong enough to bring home the championship. Cricket, the game of the spring term for the ambitious athletes, did not interest Harry. It was not a contact sport and the pace of the games was far too slow for his liking. What did come more to his attention that year at Ridley was boxing, a sport that was new to him but one which suited his competitive interests very well. Boxing was an annual winter term program which concluded with a tournament that was always eagerly awaited by the whole school. In those days, boxing was seen as a gentlemanly art and as a character builder and the coaching, mainly from ex-army instructors, was excellent. After a long process of training and preparation during physical education classes, an evening of preliminaries was followed by an evening of finals with the best boxers going at it. The bouts were closely supervised and the gloves were oversized so injuries were very rare although some mothers in the audience for the finals were always reported as nervous.

Red got through the preliminaries that first year and one of his contemporaries remembers him on the night of the finals punching away on the radiator for a warm-up before going over to the gymnasium. Red had been paired with Jack Millidge who was a year younger than himself but a boxer with considerable promise — he would later become Canadian amateur welter-weight champion. The bout between Millidge and Foster was reported as the most exciting of the evening. It was long remembered by all who were present that night, especially since its intensity necessitated a fourth round instead of the usual three. The boys completed the four rounds despite the fact that in the second round Millidge broke his left thumb and Foster sprained his wrist. The two were roundly praised for their fine exhibition of boxing and hard hitting. The whole affair was immortalised in verse by a contemporary:

When the boys of Bishop Ridley
Go a-scrapping in the ring
You're bound to see a battle
That will make your pulses sing.
Just a very short three minutes
But they make a lengthy round
In which Walker hits McCallum
And McCallum hits the ground.
And then there's Battling Greening,
That Fourth Form "kid" so fair
Who could not possibly forget
To brilliantine his hair!
Jack Millidge and Red Foster
Put up a fight so rare,
That we could only grip our seats
And look ahead and stare.

Red was learning to take care of himself in a gentlemanly way. Many of the boys who fought in the Ridley boxing square would remain the best of friends for a lifetime and many too would show up later at various stages of Red's own life.

Another highlight of 1923 was the donation of a battery powered radio set to the school. This newfangled device allowed the masters and a few senior boys to listen to the World Baseball Series in October of that year. Listeners had to be limited of course, because there were only two sets of earphones. This gift was the occasion of much excitement at the school and Harry recalled later his disappointment in not being one of the privileged senior boys!

Harry's first year at Ridley was a tremendous success in a number of areas. Although his grades were not especially good, he had registered good conduct commendation from the faculty and, partly because of his sporting abilities, had built a special relationship with Headmaster Griffith. Red had withstood the discipline imparted by the senior boys and he had absorbed the lessons that a private school offers outside its classrooms—lessons in comradeship, good manners, sportsmanship, and how to have good fun. Indeed,

RIDLEY COLLEGE—UPPER SCHOOL

Name Foster, H.G.   Form VB

Report of Progress and Conduct for the Term ending April 12th, 1924.

SUBJECT	NO. OF BOYS IN FORM	RANK IN CLASS WORK	RANK IN EXAM.	PER CENTAGE	REMARKS	MASTER
READING						
SPELLING						
ENG. GRAMMAR						
ENG. COMPOSITION	17	=12	=4	63	Exam would redeem a very poor term	R86
ENG. LITERATURE	16	15	12	28	a little better towards term end	B
ORAL COMPOSITION	18	3			Very good speaker indeed	B
ARITHMETIC						
ALGEBRA	17	17	17	0	Weak	HCA
GEOMETRY	17	16=	16=	0	very weak	HCA
TRIGONOMETRY						
LATIN						
GREEK						
FRENCH	16	11	13	15	a very poor result on elementary form work	R86
GERMAN						
ANCIENT HISTORY	14	14			Gave up trying	B
HISTORY	17	14	10	33	Made a wee effort at the end	
GEOGRAPHY						
WRITING						
DRAWING						
SCRIPTURE	17	8=	7	52	Very creditable: works well	W26
PHYSICS	16	14	10	42	Has improved	HB
CHEMISTRY	6	3	1	75		
MUSIC						
CONDUCT					Excellent	

School Re-opens April 22nd, 1924.

H C Griffith Principal.

Harry Foster's report card from April 1924.

many of Foster's characteristics were moulded further at Ridley and they would stand him in good stead in later years. He excelled in both football and hockey in his first year; he was seen as somewhat of a rising star not only in these two sports but also in boxing and, with his fine adolescent voice, in singing.

Harry's second year at Ridley was not as successful on the athletic front as the first had been. The football and the hockey teams were both runners-up for the championships, and in the annual boxing tournament Harry was eliminated in the preliminaries. There were, however, triumphs on other fronts. In September of 1923, Harry was chosen to sing the first solo in the newly built memorial chapel. Later that term, he took part in the Dramatic Society's production of *The Major's Mistake*. Harry was Victor Dubois, a Frenchman. The yearbook reviewer noted that while Harry Foster had "the obviously amusing part, he did it very well. His mannerisms and broken English brought down the house." The casting was perfect, since Harry's classroom French was horrible.

Not only was his French horrible, so were most of his other subjects. Harry himself recalled later that he set new records for poor scholarship that year. His April report reads; English composition, 14th out of 17 boys; English literature, 15th out of 16 ; Algebra, 17th out of 17, with a remark by the master "weak"; Geometry, 16th out of 17, "very weak"; French 11th out of 16, "a very poor result"; Ancient History 14th out of 14, "gave up trying"; Modern History, 14th out of 17. He did stand 3rd in a class of 18 in Oral Composition (public speaking), and 8th out of 17 in Scripture. Although Harry could think on his feet, the end of his Ridley career was clearly not far off. Harry's weak academic performance and his fun loving and sports-minded nature led one of his contemporaries to remark that if there had been a vote that year to determine the student least likely to succeed, it would have been Harry Foster!

As we now know for certain, success in life is not always wrapped up with scholarly accomplishments. Harry's parents undoubtedly hoped for better academic performance for they, like many, saw good grades as the key to university and certain professional careers. Going on to university, however, was not all that common yet even in the prep schools and it was certainly not universally taken for granted in the 1920's. Harry's grandfather, father and uncle had all obviously done well for themselves without university training. In Harry's two years at Ridley College, his mind was clearly and almost always on things other than academics. Helen and Daniel Foster might have been comforted with the knowledge that their son had developed some characteristics that would be as important, if not even more important, than high marks. He enjoyed being with people, he saw humour in most situations, he was never known to be at a loss for words and he could carry on a mature conversation with anyone. There was an adolescent charm about his manner that endeared him to staff and fellow students alike. Most important, Harry Foster was an honest individual. Pranks yes, but deceit never! These traits were as much a credit to Harry's parents as to the school.

One story from Harry's final year, illustrating his fun-loving nature, involved his Toronto friends during the Easter break. The group of friends hired a limousine one evening and took some girls to the theatre, followed by ice cream afterwards — "in other words, a riotous time." They then took the girls home and headed to the King Edward Hotel to visit one of the Ridley boys who was staying there, expecting to stay the night with him. When that did not work out, they headed back towards Oaklands Avenue. Harry, however, had told his mother that they would be staying at Aunt Lily's house that night but, since it was too late to barge in on her and too late to be getting home, they took refuge in the garage behind Harry's house and slept under a pile of burlap bags. In the morning they snuck out, got onto the streetcar and arrived at Aunt Lily's in time for breakfast. This, according to Harry's friend who remembered it, fulfilled the letter of the law if not the spirit, thus proving Red's basic honesty!

The social highlight of the final term at Ridley was the annual Cadet Ball. Girls, mostly from the Toronto girls' schools, were imported by train, carefully chaperoned and housed in the infirmary. The swimming pool was drained for a sitting area and the gymnasium was festooned with decorations done by the boys themselves. Harry chose to invite the daughter of the local minister. He had picked her up on foot to bring her to the Ball but, as the evening ended, a pelting rainstorm caused a problem. Since she was a minister's daughter, he felt that getting her back on time was the proper course of action. Not waiting for the rain to end, he quietly went over to Dr. Griffith's garage, drove the Headmaster's car over to the gymnasium and returned his

date to her home in dry condition. The next morning Dr. Griffith noticed that his tires were muddy and that tracks by the gym looked suspiciously like they were made by his car. He quickly deduced that Harry had "borrowed" the car. Harry never did tell anyone what "The Griff" did to him except to say that "he didn't cane me!" implying that Dr. Griffith rather admired his initiative.

Unfortunately the good conduct, charm and promising sporting abilities could not convince the Ridley faculty that his pre-university year would be anywhere near a success. Harry was 19 years old and both parents and school agreed that it was time to move on. Red Foster was awarded no prizes on his final Prize Day in June of 1924, but he later recalled hearing Sir Arthur Currie, the great Canadian Army Commander and keynote speaker that day, utter these prophetic words:

> . . . *The great majority of you are not prizewinners. Prizes are incentives to work, but they are not the object of work . . . Do not think that because you did not win, you have failed or that your struggle has not availed [you]. . . Most of the great poets and artists, most of the successful business men have struggled with difficulties and have wrought out of their conditions their success. . . .*

Harry left Ridley in June, 1924 with fond memories and life long friendships, but few academic credentials. It would be in areas other than academics that he would make his mark. He would return many times in the next fifty years to maintain contact with the traditions of the school, with the faculty that knew him, and especially with his friend and mentor, Dr. Harry Griffith. The stamp of the school had been placed upon him. Its Latin motto, "May I Be Consumed In Service" had taken root. Interestingly, but not surprisingly, he was invited back to Ridley to be the Prize Day speaker in June, 1973, almost fifty years after his own departure. Avoiding academic matters, his speech to the graduates emphasized the importance of service in life.

Chapter Three
The Sporting Life

For a nineteen year old who is not planning a university career, there is usually only one thing to do and that is to find a job and work for a living. In the fall of 1924, Harry's uncle Edward helped in securing Harry's first employment at the T. Eaton Company on Yonge Street, in the piece goods department. This was a very junior position involving pushing a truck from department to department, but it was experience in merchandising and it was in the real world. The fact that the Eaton Company had a hockey team in the old Mercantile League may have had some bearing on Harry's getting the job. The benefit from Harry's point of view was that it permitted him to help pay for his room and board at home and at the same time keep himself in the whirl of amateur sports where he felt most at ease.

The 1920's was truly the decade of the amateurs, and many have called those years the Golden Age of Canadian sport. In most sports the coaching and the competition were excellent, and the best athletes rolled from sport to sport over the course of the year. Red himself had done just that all of his adolescent life. In the days just prior to the advent of professional hockey, most of Canada's sporting figures were raw amateurs and they liked it that way. There was still a stigma attached to any professional (i.e., one who made money from sport) and although this would soon disappear, many athletes of the 1920's clung to their amateur status, seeing it as a symbol of what true sport was all about.

For any Toronto native, a typical boyhood dream was to play football for the Senior Argonauts. True to this form, Harry began his climb to the big team with two seasons of apprenticeship on the Junior squad. Leadership, spirit and enthusiasm for the game earned him the captain's title in his second season, as well as the 1925 Ontario Rugby Football Union Junior Championship. It was then on to the Senior Argonauts for the 1926 and 1927 seasons, and a boy's dream seemed to be unfolding. Red was a good halfback and team player, but he was not a superstar. While he had some productive games, he found himself on the bench much of the time as a substitute. Aside from his recollection of the hardness of the bench, his most vivid memory of his stay with the Senior Argos came from his very first game with the big squad. It was in Hamilton and the Argos were down by a few points when the coach finally put him into the game. He took up his position on the ten yard line as the Tigers were ready to kick. The ball spiralled overhead and the Tigers swarmed through the Argo line. As the ball arched towards his outstretched hands, a roar went up from the crowd. Harry's great moment had arrived. In his very first big league game, with stardom an imminent probability, Red Foster dropped the ball!

In the amateur hockey world of the same period, Harry did become a full time player and the three winter months were taken up as usual with a variety of teams. His first season with the T. Eaton Company ended with a city championship in the Mercantile League. This was followed by a season with the Toronto Canoe Club and a Junior Ontario Hockey Association (OHA) championship. It was then on to the St. Mary's Saints of Toronto in the Senior OHA, in a season which also ended with a provincial championship in 1927. In the memories of players from that team, their chief claim to fame was the defeat of coach Conn Smythe's Varsity Grads, winners of the Allan Cup in 1926. Red Foster played his usual centre position on the second

The T. Eaton Company Hockey Team of 1925. Harry Foster is in the back row, fifth from the left.

line and, while few goals were reported, his scrappy form of play earned him more than his share of penalties. The St. Mary's Saints became the Toronto Marlboros in 1927, and so it was as a Marlboro that Harry also spent the 1927-1928 season under the direction of coach/manager Frank Selke.

The records of the Marlboro team in the Toronto press are slim during these years. The great popularity of Senior Amateur hockey had peaked in Toronto by 1926; OHA hockey was beginning to take a back seat to the excitement generated by the rapid expansion of the National Hockey League into the United States, and by the growing local interest in the Toronto St. Patricks, newly reorganized by Conn Smythe. NHL expansion had brought with it a scramble among owners for the services of good players anywhere and Harry Foster's abilities as a centre man were certainly well known to his coach Frank Selke who also served Conn Smythe as right hand man in charge of scouting, publicity and programs. One day after a game in February 1928, Selke began to pursue Harry to consider the possibility of turning professional. Harry long remembered that moment with Selke in the corridor of the old Mutual Street Arena as one of those turning points in his life which failed to turn. He often wondered ever after what would have happened if he had jumped into the big league at that time.

There is no doubt that Harry considered the prospects of a professional hockey career seriously. There was a mystique surrounding the large salaries being paid to hockey players, and the possibility of fame and fortune would be an attraction for any twenty-three year old with decent skills. By the rules of the day, however, committing himself to the ranks of the professionals would destroy his amateur status and Red's true passion was undeniably football. As he and his father considered the options, two developments in 1928 made the decision not to turn professional an easy one. First, Uncle Edward Foster was expanding his wholesale dry goods business in Toronto and had agreed to take Harry on as an agent. This would end the brief Eaton's job and be the beginning of a potentially more lucrative sales career.

Harry as a Toronto Marlboro, 1928.

Harry Foster (back row, fourth player from the left) in a team picture for the Stobie, Forlong & Company Hockey Team.

Harry would procure new textile accounts for Uncle Edward and use Edward's office as a base for a promotions agency of his own, selling advertising for printed sports programs. Secondly, some of Harry's friends from the Balmy Beach Football Club were urging him to leave the Argos and join Toronto's east end team for a shot at winning another Grey Cup. Harry was excited about the possibilities of both developments. The idea of a professional hockey career became a thing of the past.

The decision not to turn professional was not the end of his hockey career, however. Harry spent two more winter seasons in the amateur ranks with the Stobie, Forlong &

Company team of the Standard Stock and Mining Exchange League which won the championship in 1929. This league was renowned at the time for both booze and betting. For Harry, it was good freewheeling hockey the way he liked it, rough and tumble, limited travel, plenty of fun and always great partying after the games. In his second year with Stobie, Forlong & Company, he also helped organize the National Yacht Club Sea Fleas Hockey Team of the OHA, acting as both player and coach. In 1931, Harry went back to the Toronto Marlboros, this time as manager.

As a player and as a coach, Red's heart was always in the amateur ranks where he believed that the real fun existed.

Harry, standing at the far right, as coach of the Norway Beavers, 1930. His coaching partner and good friend, Jimmy Keith, is second from the left.

In March 1930, Red's team, the National Sea Fleas, lost out in the play-offs but, as Ted Reeve wrote, it was "heartening to see two such splendid teams in action in the amateur ranks after the wholesale professional raiding." Harry Foster may have been discovering around 1930 that encouraging others to put forth effort and to rise to some sort of greatness themselves was almost as much fun as playing the games himself. Reeve concluded his description of that last play-off game by noting that "with Red Foster, the Boy Admiral, waving them on from the quarterdeck, the gallant Seamen [National Sea Fleas] put up an attack that was a masterpiece of fighting spirit." There is no doubt that Harry's competitive nature made him want to win, but how one played the game was always an equally important consideration. The coaching roles gave him opportunities to share his time and his talent with the players coming along from below and, unwittingly, to infect them with his personal brand of enthusiasm for good clean action. These abilities became apparent in hockey but would be even more evident on the football scene.

It was the call of football with Balmy Beach in the fall of 1928 which, in the end, proved to be the strongest magnet in Harry's life. In the "blue and gold" Harry Foster had certainly found a team that matched his temperament. The Beaches was founded in 1924 by men who played as much for the fun of playing as for winning. Practices were held on the old Broadview field. They had no clubhouse to call their own and, like other amateurs, all of the team members held down various jobs in the city and did their practising after work. They were a bunch of friends who protected one another on the field and off. Between 1924 and 1930, gridiron legends of the Ontario Rugby Football Union such as Ernie Crowhurst, Alex Trimble, Ted Reeve, Ab Box, Jimmy Keith, Frank Commins, and Alex Pontin captured no less than five league titles and two Grey Cups.

As the new halfback and therefore the ball carrier in 1928, Red Foster found himself almost constantly in the limelight. These were the days when helmets were optional and Red rarely wore one, a fact which accented his visibility. Players also went the full sixty minutes unless injured. Nearly six feet tall and weighing 175 pounds at the time, he was tremendously fast on his feet. He could run the ball and make amazing gains or he could plough straight through the line taking the blockers with him. Harry was also a powerful cog in the Beaches' secondary defence, always tackling hard and breaking up plays of the opposition. With his trademark red hair flying, Harry Foster became a great crowd favourite.

All of the sportswriters gave Harry plenty of ink. One typical account from 1929 in *The Toronto Star*, written by sports columnist Lou Marsh, describes the action well:

> *[Harry] grabbed the first punt from the Ottawa backfield and ran it back for a ten yard gain. Then quarterback Ponton handed him the pill for a dash at the line and Red went in all elbows and knees. And from then on the boy with the sun-burned hair was the centre of the crowd's attention. Defensively, he was in on every down, and when they gave him the ball he fought like a fiend to advance it. Not once but half a dozen times, he finished his play staggering along with a couple of husky Ottawans draped around his ears. He was such a bundle of barbed wire, and created such havoc in the enemy ranks that the boys in red made a dead set on him . . . Red didn't say a word. He just bided his time. That time came when a free-for-all started and for a minute or two the field was a maelstrom of flying fists and struggling figures . . . Anyway, Foster's maroon plume was the battle centre all afternoon and he was the outstanding star of a good team. Foster came out of the fray with a busted nose. That is the fourth time the Foster beezer has been in splints during the rugby season — but he got a well-earned touchdown on a wild-eyed buck through the line so the busted beak is regarded as a mere incident in Foster's eventful life.*

In some of the games which were reported, Red was often described as a "human bomb," a journalist's nickname which, perhaps fortunately, did not stick!

In today's age of professional dedication to a single sport, it is hard for modern readers to realize that football

The Balmy Beach Football Club, Grey Cup champions of 1930, pose for a team picture after their win. Harry is in the middle of the centre row holding the football. Ted Reeve is to his right.

in the late 1920's was only one of a number of things going on in the lives of most players. It was sometimes difficult to fit practices into their schedules and in this Harry Foster was no exception. The summer of 1930 was a particularly busy one for Harry and it was not until mid September that he actually got to his first practice. He was still working for Uncle Edward down on Wellington Street and, although he had secured a few new textile accounts after joining the business, his best efforts were evidently elsewhere and he often wondered later "how Uncle Edward put up with" him. Harry was also driving racing boats on the waterfront and selling advertising for the new sports programs he was creating at the Canadian National Exhibition. On top of these activities, he was now coaching football in the Junior ORFU league; practises and games on the Riverdale flats consumed considerable time.

Harry shared his coaching duties with his Beaches line mate Jimmy Keith, and the two of them were often absent from their own practices because of this. As the season wore on, Ted Reeve, the reporter for *The Telegram* and fellow player, was led to worry that, "Beaches might lose a match one of these days through over-anxiety of some of their players to dash off before full time and reach a phone to see how their [other] teams are doing!" This was a direct reference to Red.

Reeve had every right to be concerned about any distractions among the players that fall because he believed that his team was "on the way up." Although Balmy Beach had won its first Grey Cup in 1927, it was not until 1930, after considerable rebuilding, that a few analysts (including Reeve) saw the team as strong enough to have a chance to repeat. The regular season of 1930 ended in November with a record of five wins and one loss in official games. The semi-final game against Hamilton was an 8 to 5 victory making Balmy Beach the eastern ORFU champions. Red suffered an injury in this game and did not practice at all in the week prior to the Grey Cup final. Instead, he underwent two treatments each day for torn leg muscles at the trainer's office on Danforth Avenue. There was no way that he was

Harry Foster practicing with the Balmy Beach Football Club, the 1930 Grey Cup Champions.

going to miss participating in the Grey Cup Final!

Saturday, December 6th, dawned in Toronto with a mixture of cold and light mist that persisted all day. The Regina Roughriders, the western champions, were rated almost evenly with Balmy Beach. What the fans saw in the contest at Varsity Stadium that afternoon was described as a titanic struggle in a mud bowl shrouded in fog. Ted Reeve reported that:

When the players trotted out for the warming up exercises, they made a fine picture in colours that clashed, but five minutes after the game began, there were no colours left. In the massed plays, some of the grid men must have almost suffocated. There was mud to the left, mud to the right, and mud all around.

It took just over two hours of slopping through that mud for Balmy Beach to capture victory with an 11 to 6 score. From the Beach's perspective, it was a game that featured a total team effort and was described as such in the press, although Red Foster was named as "a tower of strength all afternoon as he smashed that western line." Reeve too was something of a hero as he entered this his last game before retirement with his arm in a sling; he still managed to put forth a strong effort on the line in the game's dying minutes.

The post victory celebrations were long remembered by the team members. There were parties at Columbus Hall on the Danforth, a community dance at the Balmy Beach Club, and medals and crests handed out at the local Beach Theatre by the owners. Unfortunately, however, some of the steam had been taken out of the celebrations by the effects of the first year of the Depression. The crowd for the 1930 Grey Cup was estimated at only about 4000 fans even though both the Junior and the Senior titles were played that same day at Varsity Stadium. Attendance was in fact far below average. This led Ted Reeve to complain shortly after that "they had won a championship with about as much fuss over it in their own home town as if they had won the relay race at the Sunday school picnic." The economic uneasi-

Small boats, known as "sea fleas," were a popular racing attraction in Toronto Harbour during the late 1920's and early 1930's.

ness in all quarters was beginning to show by that time. The resulting belt-tightening, however, did not seem to hinder further celebrations at 64 Wellington Street. This was Uncle Edward's office and the unofficial headquarters of the Beaches team. Celebrations there went on for a week!

The Grey Cup championship of December 1930 can be seen as the climax of the good-time years; from 1928 to 1930 must be counted as Harry Foster's most enjoyable and carefree salad days. He and his friends held down jobs which paid just enough to support their rambunctious life style and although there were girls involved in the fun too, none were taken too seriously at this time. It was the football and the hockey boys who would often whoop it up in post game or post practice festivities at their favourite establishments, Child's Restaurant on King Street, Bowles Restaurant at Bay and Queen streets, and the King Edward Hotel. This was the period when many legends of Harry's silliness as a brawler and a gregarious fun-loving spirit were born.

Whether or not the stories were completely true, most people later agreed that they were typical of the actions of this apparently carefree and unattached sportsman. On one occasion Red turned a whole salad bowl over a patron's head in a dispute over seating, which caused a fight right in the restaurant. Another time, a fire hose was unravelled and there was some hearty spraying of the traffic on Queen Street. At the King Edward, one famous story included Red swinging from the chandeliers and quickly being evicted. Prohibition had come to an end in Ontario in 1927 and there is no doubt that the good times enjoyed by Red and his friends were assisted by the fresh availability of alcohol. Another tale, this one unverified, tells of a Toronto streetcar piloted down the tracks by Red and the gang, with the driver in hot pursuit on foot. It seems that they were heading for Balmy Beach the easy way.

In all of the tales, there never seems to be an outcome beyond the deeds themselves; they did some things which today would get them arrested. At that time, the boys were seen by most as "characters" with no malicious intent. They were young men pursuing a good time, all the time. The fact that Red Foster always seemed to be at the centre of the action gives us some indication of his ability to cultivate a wide circle of friends who enjoyed being with him.

Red always enjoyed the opportunities later in his life when he crossed paths with the boys of yesteryear. When they met on one occasion or another, there would always be a few laughs over the pranks, in language that was a bit different from that of the business and social world which Harry adopted in the years after Balmy Beach. The support that they continued to have for each other in the ups and downs of their individual careers was remarkable. That support even extended into the next generation with each other's children.

One other story which Red revealed long after leaving the business world illustrates the fun, the petty larceny and the mutual support (of a kind) which was so characteristic of those salad days. This was the occasion in the late 1920's when Jimmy Keith of the Balmy Beach team missed a party. On one particular New Year's Eve, Foster and Keith, Frank Commins and Ernie Crowhurst, determined to get themselves into the Ballroom of the King Edward Hotel to enjoy the meal and the festivities. They had good suits but no money for such things. Between them, they rented one room in the hotel for the night and proceeded to have a party of their own.

As the clock on the Canada Life Building inched its way toward midnight, they decided that it was time to head for the big party downstairs. Closing the door behind them, they quickly realized that one of them had left the key inside. Jimmy Keith, the smallest of the little group of football friends, was conscripted to climb back inside by way of the transom, the little angled vent above each of the hotel doors of those days. The three others hoisted Keith up and pushed and prodded his barrel-chested frame as hard as they could. Half way through, Keith got stuck; he couldn't move forward or backward. With the clock now showing 11:55, they decided to abandon Keith and make their move on the Ballroom.

Since the door to the grand salon was guarded by a portly ticket taker, they headed for the kitchen. Just after the clock struck midnight and all the noise erupted, the waiters emerged carrying the fixings of the midnight feast. Behind three of these waiters, each laden with a giant tray of Chicken-à-la-King, was a smiling football player pretending to be part of the staff. Quickly blending into the crowd, they proceeded to enjoy the meal and the rest of the evening. As for Jimmy Keith, he hung in the transom for almost an hour before the house detective got him extricated. Since he could not get into the Ballroom the way the others had, and was suffering from sore ribs, he had no option but to go to bed. He was not amused at the time, but they all laughed about the incident for years!

The fact that Harry juggled two major sports successfully from 1924 through 1930 attests to the intensity of his interest, his energy and his ability. His contemporaries, men such as Lionel Conacher, Joe Primeau, Red Story, and Ted Reeve, were famous for doing the same thing, although Lionel Conacher, the hero of so many, did turn professional in 1925. Many of the amateurs, including Harry, also kept in shape each spring and summer with Canada's national sport, lacrosse. The famous Maitlands, based in Cottingham Square, his old stamping ground, was Harry's team and another source of fun and fellowship with the boys.

Yet another sport had made its appearance on the Toronto scene in early 1928 and it soon became another ingredient in Harry's life — motor boat racing. The sport originated on Florida's flat waterways in 1926 and quickly caught on. The idea arrived in Canada in the spring of 1928 mostly through the efforts of Lou Marsh, the sports writer for *The Toronto Star*, who saw in it a risky, thoroughly exciting and somewhat glamorous activity for local boat enthusiasts and spectators alike. Marsh persuaded the National Yacht Club to provide spaces for the boats and to promote races for these small hydroplanes, soon popularly known as sea fleas. Here was a new activity tailor-made for the likes of Harry Foster. The fact, as he admitted, that he "didn't know the difference between a rowboat and a

Harry Foster (on right) stands with his boat mechanic, Gowan Scarlett, at the National Yacht Club, Toronto, in 1929 or 1930.

Chinese junk before he started in it" was quite immaterial. This water sport promised opportunities for great fun, an element of danger and plenty of camaraderie.

Harry was not long in throwing himself into the excitement as a member of the National Yacht Club. In the late 1920's, the outboard motor was emerging from an unreliable toy into a regular means of propulsion. Boat builders and engine manufacturers were eager to test their engines in competition. In the first couple of years at least, with a developing eye for promotion, Harry made good use of free equipment in return for hard testing.

The sea fleas themselves came in many shapes and sizes. They ranged from three to four metres in length and weighed about 45 kilograms. Except for the small and fragile deck, they were almost all cockpit. The heavy engines were clamped onto a wide stern board and the drivers had to crouch as far forward as they could in order to prevent the boats from sinking stern first. The most popular engine was the mighty Johnson four-cylinder which boasted the highest propulsion available at that time, almost 60 kilometres per hour! The fragile nature of the craft led to numerous upsets and the Toronto Life Saving Service

Harry pilots the boat that he would enter in the 1928 World Sea Fleas Championship held in the Toronto harbour. The Canadian National Exhibition ground's Princess Gate is in the background.

was in constant demand at races. These little craft would literally fly across the water, and in rough weather they would hop from wave to wave exerting bone crushing force on the drivers. The sea fleas sported fitting nicknames such as *Bronco-busters*, *Leaping Lenas*, *Puddle-Jumpers*, *Water Buggies*, or *Jumpin' Bath Tubs*. Spectators by the thousands crowded the sea walls to witness the antics of the machines, and the sportswriters for all of the newspapers had a field day with their stories.

A parade of sportsmen entered into this new racing forum and Harry was at the forefront. He was elected as an officer in the motor racing section of the Yacht Club in 1928 within a month of his joining. This post gave him the opportunity to be an organizer and a boat driver at the same time. As his friend, reporter and fellow racer Lou Marsh reported, Harry went into action "with his new puddle-jumper with all the abandon with which he chased either the pigskin or the puck. When he opens her up his red hair looks like the business end of a pink meteor going someplace in an 'eluva' hurry to get there." It was in this boating atmosphere that he also met Harold Ballard the hockey promoter. Like Red, Harold had a reputation for promoting, for daring and for having a roaring good time when work was over. Foster and Ballard cemented a permanent friendship at this time and they would figure prominently in each others' lives from these days forward.

The first racing event in Canada for hydroplanes was organized on Victoria Day weekend in May of 1928. A four kilometre triangle was marked off at Sunnyside in front of the Canadian National Exhibition grounds. Medals and a silver trophy for the winner were offered by the National Yacht Club. The sea wall was packed with spectators as twelve boats turned up for the race. Two of the boats capsized before the start and, on the starting signal from the cannon at the Yacht Club, two more quickly became casualties for the Life Saving Service. Red Foster's boat, *Galloping Ghost*, took the lead almost immediately and maintained full throttle for all three required circuits. On the second lap around, the bottom planks began to crack, but he held on. Crossing the finish line as the First International Hydroplane Champion of the World, his boat simply sank beneath him!

During the first two summers of sea flea racing, Red rode the waves to both victories and defeats. At the official CNE races, he seemed always to be plagued with engine failures; he never repeated as the Sea Flea Champion. It didn't matter, however; win or lose, it was the sheer joy of racing and the good times associated with it that appealed to him. He had made a name for himself as a perpetual challenger, as a crowd pleaser, and as somewhat of a daredevil.

Red's favourite stunt was to come down full speed, jam the throttle over hard, and do a 360 degree turn on the spot. Apparently, no other driver could do it. In one practice run, however, the engine had not been properly secured and, when he ripped the boat around, the engine did a back somersault — and so did Red and the boat! With his engine at the bottom of the lake, a brief note in *The Toronto Star* observed that "Mr. Harry Foster spent Sunday on a fishing trip, on Lake Ontario. He was using a grappling iron and a magnet, but he didn't catch anything except another coat of sunburn." In 1929, a boat was produced for the CNE that would drive up a sloping platform, leap through a paper hoop and land back in the water. Harry Foster was the only driver who is reported to have attempted it, but there is no

Harry was known for his daredevil stunts on the small "sea flea'" boats, as evident in this photo which appeared in The Toronto Star *in 1928.*

record of any success.

One incident in May of 1930 was anything but fun, however, and it may have had some influence on turning Harry into a much more sober and thoughtful adult. It was a Friday evening and two National Yacht Club boating enthusiasts, Harold Ballard and Jimmy Rogers, agreed to a short test of Harry's new sea flea boat. About a kilometre out, the steering wires entangled, the boat turned the wrong way into a wave, and the three men were thrown into the frigid waters of Lake Ontario. Wearing sweaters, coats, and no life preservers, it quickly became apparent to both Foster and Ballard that Rogers, a non swimmer, was in trouble. Between the two of them they managed to keep Rogers afloat while the boat, its motor still running, circled out of control and out of reach. A sailboat from the Club saw the struggle and sped to the scene, but it was at least fifteen minutes before it could get close enough to extend a grappling pole. As Foster was dragged semi-conscious into the rescue boat, Rogers slipped from his grasp and sank. Ballard, fighting exhaustion, was also hauled aboard. Suffering the onset of hypothermia, both men waited at the yacht club while other searchers combed the site of the tragedy. When told that the search had been in vain, both men wept. What impact this event had on Foster will never be known. A life had been lost, accidentally for sure, but in the reckless pursuit of a good time.

Red's racing career continued well into the 1930's and he continued to be a key figure in the affairs of the NYC. As horsepower became more reliable, boat sizes increased. By 1932, they were into inboards with over a hundred horsepower. In 1934 Harry persuaded the CNE authorities to inaugurate the 225-cubic-inch class races on the Exhibition waterfront. Some of the beautiful mahogany craft built for that class can still be seen in Muskoka waters, north of Toronto, in the summertime. The biggest event of that 1934 summer was labelled by the CNE as an International Powerboat Race, over a fifteen mile distance and was promoted as the "Championship of the World." Ten starters, six from the United States, were attracted by the prize money, and the winner who emerged from the competition was Harold Wilson of Ingersoll, driving his *Little Miss Canada III*. Red, the chief promoter and local favourite, was the runner-up on points even though the engine in his boat, *Atom*, died in the last heat. He would always claim thereafter to have been the runner-up as World Champion! The races in 1934 were really Red's last in organized racing. The cost of ownership and maintenance, as well as exciting business affairs, eventually pushed the boating game into the realm of Red's memory.

Twenty-five years later, Ted Reeve was to recall an occasion in the late 1920's when Red had taken the sportswriter for a hair-raising spin in one of his sea fleas.

It is some time since we had a ride in front of an outboard geared to go about a mile a minute . . . Last voyage we took, in fact, was when Mr. Harry Foster was a halfback with crazy legs, glassblowers' ankles and a winning spirit that would lift an entire team out of the doldrums, showed us some of the fine points of outboard motoring and eventually went halfway up Bathurst Street in his boat when he forgot to shut off the motor while approaching the dock. We took the King Street streetcar the rest of the way home and have not been back for further demonstrations.

Ted Reeve remembered the boating days of almost a quarter of a century before because he was one of the reporters who had had a field day reporting them. He was also a skilled chronicler of football during that same period. In fact, his memories of football would be even more vivid than those of the boats because as a member of the Balmy Beach football team, Reeve would battle on the field for the full game and then dash back to his *Telegram* office and report it for the next day's edition.

The year 1930 had been eventful to say the least, with the Grey Cup Championship marking the high point in Harry's sporting career. The retirement of a number of players from the Beaches team, including that of his best friend, Ted Reeve, as well as football rule changes for 1931 involving the new forward pass, made 1930 the end of an era in many ways. Moreover, recurring pain in his ankles and knees from years of injuries, new coaching possibilities in both hockey and football, opportunities in the promotions and program business and perhaps the boating tragedy as well, all led Harry to consider new directions.

Chapter Four
On the Air

Of all the years in Canada's 20th century, 1931 would perhaps be the most difficult one in which to change the pattern of one's life in a positive direction. The nation, and the rest of the world, was sinking into the depths of the Depression. Lives were certainly changing, but all too frequently for the worse. Harry Foster's life changed directions that year too, but he managed to land squarely on his feet by making the most of the opportunities that presented themselves. He seized on these opportunities with enthusiasm and 1931 became a successful transition year in spite of the economic distress all around him. Whether it was a basic instinct for survival that forced the change, a hyperactive life style, or simply a passion for making things happen is hard to determine. Foster continued his "always-on-the-go" lifestyle as his career shifted from active sportsman to promoter of sports and promoter of the merchandise linked to it. The keys to this shift in direction are found in the fortunate combination of the interest in and the growing availability of the new medium of radio and the explosion of interest and excitement in a new sport sweeping North America — professional wrestling.

Wrestling, sometimes called the world's oldest sport, had been around in Canada for a long time. In the early part of the 20th century, it was often associated with brawls between gangs, individual fights and low life activities in general. Boxing, by contrast, was seen as the manly art of self defence and enjoyed the benefits of better facilities, better coaching, and enthusiasm from the private schools both in England and in Canada. By 1930, the roles of these two sports were beginning to reverse. The wrestling game was changing and its popularity was growing dramatically.

A promotional drawing describing the action during a wrestling match between Mr. George and Mr. Baffert. Matches of this sort were popular fare for sport fans in the early days of radio broadcasting.

The old rough and tumble tactics were giving way to what we now recognize as theatrics. Combinations of combat, speed, acrobatics and showmanship were beginning to fill the wrestling halls with enthusiastic crowds. As the crowds grew so too did the stable of wrestlers who moved from city to city on regular circuits.

The interest in professional wrestling was also a product of the Depression. More and more people had time on their hands and an evening's entertainment could be theirs for as little as 25 cents. Skilled match-makers could get the "grapplers," as they were called, to play to the crowds. Not unlike the ancient Roman mobs which watched the gladiators battle for life itself, the Depression crowds would howl for the defeat of the villains and cheer themselves hoarse for the victors. Skilled promoters were soon filling the Mutual Street Arena and Massey Hall in Toronto and venues in other large North American cities with fans eager to watch the weekly struggles of the gargantuan professionals, the "mat men." Then as now, whether the people attended these bouts realized that the wrestlers were merely providing exhibitions, was quite beside the point.

Riding the crest of the renewed enthusiasm for cheap spectator sports of all kinds in the early 1930's was the excitement generated by the medium of radio. Following the American lead, radio in Canada began its spectacular grass roots growth at this time. The cumbersome batteries of the 1920's sets were being replaced by electric current flowing from the wall sockets of almost every home. Radio sets themselves were cheap enough for almost every family to own, and the annual licensing fee of $2.00 was a small price for entertainment any evening of the week. In 1931, Toronto had five commercial radio stations, although none broadcast for more than a few hours each day. They vied with one another to attract listeners with appealing programming.

In the early years of the Depression, radio was seen more as a source of entertainment than of information. Its original appeal was to people of lesser means who had limited access to the more sophisticated forms of diversion which

Foster was quick to capitalize on the growing popularity of radio by linking his broadcasts to the promotion of products such as Vaseline which, in the 1930's, was advertised as a digestible throat salve.

any metropolitan area offered. Regular news broadcasts that provided the type of "every-hour-on-the-hour" news that we now take for granted, did not make their regular appearance until later in the 1930's. In short, radio in its pioneer days was an extension of live theatre. The finest talent in all fields from the entire world was becoming available to everyone simply by twisting the dial on the radio set. Without modern facilities to record programs in advance, most of the early programming was live. Aside from a great quantity of American programming already filling the air waves, there was plenty of local talent to draw on, soloists of all sorts, choirs, excellent orchestras and, of course, big dance bands.

It was natural that the broadcasting of sporting events would also begin to grow in the early 1930's, although in 1931 it was certainly not a new phenomenon. Foster Hewitt, who would long be the voice of NHL hockey, had already done his first broadcast in 1923 over CFCA, the station owned by *The Toronto Star*. What was new eight years later, however, was the firm marriage of wrestling, a scrappy form of live theatre, to commercial radio. Each helped the other to become successful. A pioneer in this endeavour and other commercial sporting broadcasts was Harry "Red" Foster.

Since the days of the Sea Fleas at the CNE beginning in 1928, Harry had obtained the rights to the various printed programs for the waterfront. This meant that he sold advertising space to clients and printed the order of events and details of the races. After 1930, Harry also had these rights in the old Mutual Street Arena; he was printing the line-ups for amateur hockey games, and the "cards" for the various wrestling bouts. A modest 10 cents per program does not sound like much, but as the crowds for the wrestling events grew, so did the size of the printed programs with their ubiquitous advertising, and Harry's profits as well. The same thing would be true for the programs at the football games. Without one of his brochures, you simply didn't know the players.

Harry was not only placing the ads in printed programs for clients, but he was also writing their content. One of his first major clients for the CNE programs had been Ewart Greig, head of the Canadian National Carbon Company's radio station CKNC. One day, early in 1931, Greig told Harry that his knowledge of sports, the new field of broadcasting and his ability to create advertising copy, should somehow be brought together. Since Foster Hewitt had the hockey programs in the new Maple Leaf Gardens wrapped up, Harry reasoned that the next best thing would surely be the wrestling matches at the Mutual Street Arena. Greig agreed.

CKNC quickly prepared to put wrestling on the air with the purchase of a new remote carbon microphone and a telephone line to the Arena. Nervousness, of course, was never an issue. Harry prepared for the airing of the commercials for National Carbon's "Eveready Batteries," and he consulted with the promoter on the finer points of wrestling. With his advertising scripts in hand, Harry E. Foster made his inaugural broadcast of the bout between Ed, "the Strangler" Lewis and Stanley Stasiak, "the Pitiless Pole" from a ringside seat on April 11, 1931.

Judging from the response in the Toronto papers the next day, the broadcast was a smashing success. From Harry's point of view, the triumph was more a learning experience than anything else. First, as he freely admitted, he really didn't know a crotch hold from a strangle hold. Secondly, he quickly realized that sports casting was more than just a matter of charm and a personal interest in sports. Fortunately, his good friend Ted Reeve, *The Telegram's* brilliant sports writer and an avid fan of wrestling himself, accompanied Harry on that first venture and spent most of his time scribbling notes for Red to read. When the wrestlers got themselves into a head lock and simply lay on the canvass doing nothing in particular, it took some very quick Foster wit to pound his hand on the mat near the microphone to simulate action for the listeners. Over the course of the next few bouts, Harry devised a number of sound effects to sharpen the picture for the home audience.

It was not long before other stations were asking for

Harry's new found expertise. When Henry Gooderham's CKGW first ventured into the field within a month of the CKNC inaugural broadcast, the station cautiously solicited reader response through the newspapers. Dozens of letters poured in, all apparently favourable. One typical listener wrote that "living on Centre Island with no boat after 8:00 pm, Red sure made a great job on the broadcast; in fact he made me jump a couple of times. I could see the wrestler falling on top of me." And Ted Reeve wrote, somewhat prophetically,

. . . the broadcast must have been even better than it sounded from where we were sitting. The letters are pouring in telling how much Red Foster's efforts as a McNamee [the most famous American sportscaster of the day] were appreciated throughout the province, and if the Redhead can get by on a wrestling bout, he should be able to go big at anything else in the radio announcing line. He can rush through the adjectives like he can through a football line. Attaboy Red, old boy, old boy, oh boy. . . .

The wrestling success was indeed the foothold upon which Red Foster would build his broadcasting career. It was not long before he was into freelance sports broadcasting almost full time.

Red's seizing of the opportunities in broadcasting was a classic case of both being at the right place at the right time and being blessed with sincere interest in what he was doing and the natural talent to do it well. He developed a gift for

Hundreds of swimmers participate in a marathon swim at Toronto Harbour. Harry Foster's early radio broadcasting career got its start covering events such as this.

Harry Foster interviewing the winner of a marathon swim.

painting pictures with words, and for putting the very essence of the sports contests into the homes of his listeners. Equally important, his distinct and resonant voice did its work with an infectious enthusiasm which captured the hearts of a wide listening audience.

Nor was his talent in these areas lost on his commercial clients. They were quick to understand the value of the promotion of various products through sports casting and they wished to reap the dividends. In Harry's presentations on the air, there was little difference between the excitement on the field or on the mat and the excitement of smoking an R. G. Dunn cigar or using Castrol Motor Oil! Some critics of commercial radio in the early 1930's saw the mixture of sports and advertising as terribly crass, but Harry saw it only as a marvellous opportunity which could

be pursued for the benefit of everyone involved.

While wrestling had been at the beginning of things in April 1931, Harry's first year behind the microphone saw him doing OHA hockey from the Mutual Street Arena, lacrosse and baseball from the old Maple Leaf Stadium on Toronto Island, the marathon swims at the Canadian National Exhibition, and of course, football from a number of venues. Late in November, Ted Reeve noted that Red had broadcast three hockey games in the same week and "they all went 20 or 30 minutes extra by which time Foster had skated himself into a whisper." In covering the football season of 1931 on the air rather than on the field, Harry's heart must have been in both places at the same time. If his ankles could no longer stand the strain, his voice certainly did.

In November 1931, Harry would claim to have made the first coast to coast broadcast of a football contest. Only a year earlier, he had been sloshing around in the mud himself on the field. The 1931 game originated at Molson Stadium in Montreal and looped its way to station CKGW in Toronto and then beyond. Because the network hook-ups were so scattered however, it did not blanket the country, but it did crackle its way through on telephone lines to receivers in Vancouver and Sydney, Nova Scotia. Harry would claim another Foster first.

The Grey Cup final in November 1934, between Sarnia and Regina which Harry broadcast from Varsity Stadium in Toronto, did have complete network coverage and should be the real date of the first truly coast-to-coast broadcast of the Fall Classic. From the rooftops of various stadiums during the 1930's, Harry's distinctive voice became "the voice of big league football," and of many other sports as well.

Harry thrived in his new active life in the broadcasting business. He cultivated new acquaintances in the sports world, travelled often to broadcasting sites outside of Toronto, and still maintained a hearty contact with the old football crowd at various watering holes in the city.

The variety of jobs which he undertook were not without

Harry stood in the background during his pioneer broadcast of the King's Plate horse race in 1931 where the winning owner, R.W.R Cowie (Froth Blower was the winning horse) stands with Palmer Right, Ontario Jockey Club Sececretary, Governor General Lord Bessborough, and OJC Director, George Beardmore.

their difficulties however. Broadcasting conditions in outdoor stadiums had improved somewhat from the earliest days, but heavy equipment still had to be lugged to the rooftop for each engagement. There were numerous times when he got soaked by rain or frozen by the cold, and there was nothing to do except stay at his post until the game was over. Reminiscing years later, he remembered vividly the early 1930's as the days before comfortable press boxes, noting that, "I'd often be lying flat on my belly on some rooftop in sub zero weather pouring out non-stop commen-

tary — and dying to go to the john."

Advertising copy for the events also had to be written and arranged. The artists (usually soloists or small bands) also had to get themselves up with Harry, onto the rooftops or into the rafters or wherever, for their short intermission performances. At the wrestling matches, if the referee handed down an unpopular decision, Harry was frequently in the line of fire, usually thrown wads of paper. Once, a bottle hurled from the crowd smashed only inches from his head. When he introduced the Midget Car Races to the

A cartoon drawn by one of Harry's friends pokes fun at the rudimentary conditions under which the early broadcasts of football games were made.

CNE, the noise of the engines threw the radio station temporarily off the air.

Far worse, however, was Harry's speculation on the success of Midget Car racing. He thought he had the world by the tail after reaping an $1800 profit on the first night's operation. A couple of accidents and a rainy night later, Red recalled, he was broke and right back where he started. For Harry, the problems were learning experiences and simply went with the territory.

Early in 1932, he began a regular biweekly radio feature called "Sporting Aces." This name was undoubtedly a take-off on his friend Ted Reeve's regular *Telegram* column called "Sporting Extras." Harry's "Sporting Aces" would last most of the decade and it eventually enjoyed a wide audience by way of multi-station loops all over Ontario. On these fifteen-minute segments, sponsored by the makers of Castrol Motor Oil, he interviewed sports personalities by the dozens. The venture into the interviewing of sports personalities was a natural broadcasting by-product but, for Harry, the inaugural interview was less than a polished one.

Two weeks after his first broadcast on April 11, 1931, Harry decided to bring two of the famous wrestlers to the CKNC station to try an interview. In their excitement to get on the air, a real novelty in those days, the two behemoths, as Harry called them, burst into the studio while another program was in progress. "Infant's Delight," was designed for mothers and featured nursery rhymes and songs for toddlers. The frightened announcer could only interrupt his program with, "Well, well, folks, we have a surprise for you! Harry Foster has just walked into the studio with Stanley Stasiak and Bibber McCoy!!!" There is no doubt that the interruption was a surprise to the mothers in the studio as well as to the listeners. It was several minutes before Harry could get the wrestlers out of the studio to wait their turn. The interview, when it did come, was reported as being "all too short."

Another sport that was ready-made both for Harry's broadcasting repertoire, and for the interviewing of the celebrities that went with it, was Six-Day Cycling. Not unlike wrestling, which captivated Depression crowds with its thrills and cheap admission prices, the Six-Day riders burst onto the Toronto sports scene in the early 1930's and lasted for most of the decade. Their races usually occurred in April after the ice was removed from the arenas. The two-man teams of "wheelmen," as the racers were called, began their gruelling circuits on the banked pine tracks after midnight on a Sunday and finished late on the following Saturday, thus preserving Ontario's legislated day of rest. With one team member in motion at all times during the 140 hours of competition, as many as 4000 kilometres would be chalked up between them.

The excitement for the fans, however, lay in the sprints

somehow smelled a rat. He stuck his finger into the bottle and the game was up. The bottle contained iodine! One can only imagine how the story would have been told years later if the trainer had succeeded in his prank. Red Foster would have had more than red hair!

If 1931 was the transition year in Harry's life from sportsman to hustling business man, the whole first half of the decade laid a solid foundation for his broadcasting career. What made Harry's career different from others who simply broadcast events was his flair for combining his sports expertise with his zeal to promote products for everyone's benefit. One early example of what might be called a budding social conscience was an amateur boxing bout which he arranged as a charity event late in 1932 at the Arena Gardens to benefit *The Telegram* Readers' Relief Fund and *The Toronto Star* Christmas Fund, both of which were an early form of privately administered poor relief.

For this event, Harry secured trophies from local business men and even donated one himself. He got two radio stations to donate the time on the air and Toronto Fuels Limited, the major sponsor, promised to give one dollar to each charity for every ton of coal ordered during the broadcast. He even talked the boys who sold the programs into giving their time free! It was the beginning of the creation of many win-win situations. The charity benefited through Harry's efforts, the people got their sports event, and the sponsors got publicity. Indeed, Harry's fondness for charitable work had its beginnings in his upbringing, but it took concrete form very early in his broadcasting career. As he prospered financially himself, his efforts in this regard grew proportionally.

There is no doubt that Harry enjoyed the on-air aspects of his work as well as the promotions side of it. He also enjoyed the many opportunities to be where the action was and to be associated closely with the big names of the day. In his coverage of the Canadian Olympic Trials in Hamilton in July 1932, for instance, he actually stood on the finish line as he relayed the action to his radio listeners and interviewed many of the competitors after their races. He

Harry became one of the best known sports broadcasters in the early days of radio from his work in such places as the Mutual Street Arena in Toronto.

loved mixing with crowds and especially with children, gathering stories and sharing with his audiences the triumphs and tragedies of sportsmen of all kinds.

The increasing exposure on radio encouraged Harry to become more conscious of his public image. He had been told, in fact, by Ewart Greig of the Canadian National Carbon Company just before his debut with wrestling that, if he wanted to be a success, he could not expect to be on the sports pages and the business pages at the same time. He had to choose one or the other.

One incident from the fall of 1932 suggests that he was at least aware of his reputation, as he told the story anyway. Harry wanted to see the great Harmsworth Boat Race in Detroit and talked *The Telegram* into sending him as their correspondent and into footing the bills. With him on the trip was the reporter for *The Mail & Empire* and good friend, Ken McTaggart. Harry also took his mother along to give her a bit of a break from her responsibilities at home. Upon arrival in Detroit, with his mother safely in the hotel, Ken and Harry went looking for a Canadian beer in the Prohibition-bound city.

They ended up above a restaurant in a seedy part of town which turned out to be more of a brothel than a pub. Just as the boys were about to quench their thirsts, the bartender shouted, "It's the Purple Gang" [apparent rivals of that establishment]. Everybody dove for cover. The bartender then turned out the lights and grabbed a double-barrelled shotgun. Harry said, "Let me have the gun," which the man did, seeing his patron as a man who could probably look after himself. The Canadian boys then ran down the stairs, out the back door (leaving the gun behind) and hailed a cab.

McTaggart had his headline ready the next day had they been arrested — "Area Residents Found In, Defending House of Ill Repute" but, because of the escape, he didn't include the incident in his report to the papers back home. Harry was relieved and Mrs. Foster never did find out what the two innocents had been through the night before!

Within a year of that first wrestling broadcast, Harry was finding that he could not handle all of the paper work associated with the business by himself, despite his boundless energy. This prompted him to invite his father to join what he had been calling his "agency." It was the accounting side of things that needed attention and there appears to have been enough work for Daniel to leave the wholesale hardware business behind.

This merger of talents coincided with Uncle Edward's departure from his office on Wellington Street to a new base in Montreal. Harry's connections with the textile business finally came to an end after having been tenuous for some time. The new situation was unusual — the father joined the son's business. There had always been a strong relationship between the two men. Daniel had been associated with his son in an unofficial capacity since 1929. By 1932, he was a silent partner and confidant. Harry respected his father's business wisdom and cherished even more the genuine friendship they shared. "D. H." as he was always called, gave freely of his knowledge of the business world and would remain with the agency for the rest of his life.

In 1934, with business going so well, Harry applied to incorporate. Letters Patent were sought and granted for the establishment of The Harry E. Foster Agencies Limited, specializing in printed sports programs, radio broadcasting, sound equipment, and advertising. The new company called for more office space. This led Harry to leave 64 Wellington Street and to take up space in new rooms in the MacLean Building on Dundas Street.

With all his activity in various radio studios and on location, Harry never lost sight of the fact that children were the paying fans of the future. He geared his "Sporting Aces" program in particular to the younger set, although there is no doubt that the adult audience was captivated as well. One interesting indication of Foster's popularity with young people, his wide audience, and a sign of the economic times as well, came in 1934. During a wrestling broadcast, Harry offered the first 300 boy listeners a free hockey stick autographed by Gus Sonnenberg. Five thousand replies came in by mail with over half of them postmarked the same day! Because of the demand, Red convinced the sponsors to supply 500 hockey sticks; the first 300 were signed by the wrestler and the rest by Red himself. On the Saturday following the broadcast, Red acted as host at The Toronto Radio Store on Yonge Street where the lucky winners received their prized lumber.

Broadcasting opportunities seemed to flow like water in the early 1930's despite the problems associated with the

Depression. Harry was a methodical salesman (as opposed to the high pressure sort) whose genuine enthusiasm for everything almost guaranteed success. He built upon his reputation as a promoter. In fact, the marriage he created between radio and merchandise of all sorts turned almost every broadcast, whether it was a sporting event or a special event like the Royal Winter Fair or the King's Plate horse race, into a promotion for something.

He learned quickly that creating advertising for clients could be even more profitable than selling it. Not only did he deliver advertisements over the airwaves, but he spent considerable time preparing just the right words. He had an uncanny sense of what sort of messages would best sell products. He became, in fact, a master at win-win-win situations. Harry promoted the merchandise and the clients sold more. The listeners enjoyed the entertainment (and often free prizes) and Harry reaped the financial rewards.

The 1931 shift in Harry's career direction had been a gradual one. This is suggested by his appearance at the first couple of football practices with the Balmy Beach team early in September. It was as if Harry could not quite let go of the rough and tumble camaraderie of the game. The weakened ankles, the promotions and the broadcasting

opportunities, however, had already cast the die in favour of the microphone side of the football field. His retirement from the game late in September was, in fact, forced upon him by the other irons that he himself had put into the fire since the time of his inaugural wrestling broadcast in April. Harry's decision was made public and official by his friend Ted Reeve who was led to write a lament just before the first game of the 1931 season. Fearing for the success of Balmy Beach, Reeve noted that another looked for figure on the Beach backfield

. . . will not be in uniform for instead of plunging into the scrimmage, our Harry will be plunging into one of those non-stop play by play discourses . . . through a CKNC microphone. In fact, the hard fighting, fierce tackling Pride of Ridley, may do all his broadcasting from grandstand roofs this year . . . and the gridiron will be a less stirring spot without him.

Football's loss, however, was broadcasting's gain. As the first part of the Depression decade proved, Harry Foster had simply followed his instincts for capitalizing on opportunities. The second half of the decade would build upon the first half carrying The Harry E. Foster Agencies Limited to new heights of profitability and taking Harry "Red" Foster himself to new heights of popularity and visibility. His voice in the 1930's was next only to those of Foster Hewitt and Wes McKnight in recognizability. Red's voice, his enthusiasm, his interest in children and, strangely, the birth of the Dionne Quintuplets would provide further opportunities for growth and excitement in the latter half of that busy decade.

Maple Leaf Gardens, as it looked during the 1930's.

Chapter Five
Welcome to the Club

It is hard to believe that there were many opportunities for anything in the 1930's as the world struggled with the effects of the Great Depression. In Canada, almost every business enterprise was struggling and many were in a state of collapse. Jobs were scarce, wages were abominable and people lined up for food relief everywhere. Considerable belt tightening was evident among people at all levels of society. The only exceptions were among the ranks of professional athletes, the magnates of hockey, some independent businessmen and a few tycoons; these were clearly in a minority.

Harry Foster, although no tycoon, would have been considered relatively well off during these years. He still lived at home on Oaklands Avenue, but with his ability to hustle advertising, his grip on the program rights for events at the Mutual Street Arena and the Canadian National Exhibition, and his broadcasting talents, he more than held his own. Not only did he have his own sports car but, in May 1934, he presented a new car to his father in appreciation of their business relationship. He also began to acquire property on Alcorn Avenue in the area just behind his Oaklands home. Whether or not he had expansion plans this early in his career is unknown, but properties in most areas of Toronto could be had relatively cheaply at the time, if one had the cash. These all turned out to be sound investments.

Because of the Depression, people everywhere were making do with less. No matter how hard times are, however, there will always be a need for amusement and, in those years, cheap spectator sporting events were readily available and radio provided virtually free entertainment at almost any time of day. Early thirties radio served up a steady diet of increasingly sophisticated music, sports programming and talk shows. By the later thirties, radio would be adding regular newscasts, helping to make people much more aware of the world around them. Harry Foster would play an important part in all of these activities.

Undoubtedly, one of the most spectacular news items of 1934 issued from Callander, Ontario, when the Dionne Quintuplets were born. This was an event which encouraged daily monitoring. Their birth was nothing short of a medical miracle. Their survival was the beginning of a multi-million dollar bonanza to northern Ontario as the hordes of tourists and curiosity-seekers began to haunt the Dionne homestead. Behind protective barriers, the little girls would be on public display for the first nine years of their lives. Their story was told and retold in the media, and promoters (including the Dionne parents) sold everything from toothpaste to tea towels in honour of their very existence.

Between 1934 and 1943, the quintuplets headed the list of best known international celebrities along with Charlie Chaplin, Amos 'n Andy, Donald Duck and Mickey Mouse. They were the good news on the pages of a press choked with the bad — wars in Asia, political unrest in Europe, the abdication crisis in England and frequent local headlines of fires, auto and train wrecks, strikes, marches of the unemployed and general Depression distress. It was in the promotional aspects of the quintuplet story that Harry Foster, very indirectly, became involved; this involvement would usher a new chapter into an already busy career.

By the summer of 1934, the St. Lawrence Starch Company, makers of Bee Hive Corn Syrup, was running advertisements claiming that their syrup had been fed to the Quints during their first days of struggle for survival. Canada Starch, the makers of Crown Brand Corn Syrup, protested believing that their brand was actually the one in the Dionne cupboard. Large sums of money were paid by both companies to the Dionnes for exclusive claiming rights and an inevitable lawsuit between the two companies soon followed. The judge eventually dismissed the case (which involved only a few drops of syrup anyway) but the controversy began an advertising war of sorts in the newspapers.

Late in 1934, Canada Starch called upon The Harry E. Foster Agencies with the idea of using radio as an additional means of selling their product. Harry, as might be expected, was full of suggestions. The plan that emerged involved programming aimed at boys and girls in the ten to sixteen-year-old range, the consumers of the day whom Harry believed would be the buyers of tomorrow. And who better to appeal to the minds of this youthful group than the equally youthful and enthusiastic Harry "Red" Foster himself?

Out of the negotiations and planning of early 1935, the Crown Brand Radio Sports Club was born. It was an instant success, beyond the wildest dreams of the agency. Within six months there were 10,000 members, and at its peak there would be nearly 50,000 faithful radio listeners on record. Its first broadcast took place in April 1935 over Station CRCT and the program, which aired twice each week, was destined to continue for nearly nine years. Its success was rooted in Harry's unique talents as a knowledgeable sportsman, his genuinely enthusiastic presentation of material and his ability to coax the Canada Starch Company to foot all the bills. Another long term win-win-win situation was in the making. Sales of Crown Brand Syrup skyrocketed, and Harry Foster became a legend in his own time at least in the ranks of the youth of Toronto and Ontario.

The leading feature of each Crown Brand Sports Club program was a story drawn from the world of sport. Due to his past involvement in this world, it was easy enough to come up with an endless supply of tales and anecdotes. Harry found some sort of lesson embedded in all of these and he used his stories to promote his own belief in the value of teamwork and good clean fun. By 1935, Harry also had some very capable writers on his staff who could take a tidbit of information and turn it into a five minute monologue. The rest of each program consisted of talks on such topics as life-saving, team spirit, rules of games, and how to play.

Red never seemed to mind the youthful voices which would phone his office hoping for a personal chat. He also answered questions on the air and by mail and, of course, he plugged Crown Brand Syrup at every opportunity. There was little need to plug Crown Brand as the one which was fed to the Dionne Quints; the syrup spoke for itself and the kids consumed it by the gallon if only to obtain the valuable labels. Opening each program with the tune "Anchors Aweigh" and his trademark greeting "Hello, Gang," Harry closed it with a piece of philosophy, learned at Ridley, in which he truly believed:

> *For when the One Great Scorer*
> *comes to write against your name.*
> *He writes - not that you won or lost -*
> *but how you played the game.*

While there is no doubt that Harry believed in this philosophy, and was always prepared to make an issue of it in his broadcasts, his career up to this time was based on the premise that he would win. That premise would, in fact, never change.

Membership in the Sports Club was easy; the only cost was a stamp. One simply mailed in a name and address, along with a label from a tin of Crown Brand Corn Syrup. In return, listeners got a numbered membership button which, somewhat mysteriously, was the "Open Sesame" to even greater benefits. In 1935 alone, members of the Crown Brand Sports Club were invited to attend a Six-Day bicycle race at Maple Leaf Gardens, the motorcycle races at the

CNE grounds, an International League baseball game, an Argo football game and a movie at the Uptown Theatre. Each event was free to the button wearers who brought the ever-useful Crown Brand label with them. Nearly 7,000 members turned up as non-paying guests of the Toronto Argonauts at Varsity Stadium for the game against the Montreal Wheelers in November 1935. Their cheering, orchestrated by Red, completely drowned out the 3,000 adults. Armed with free programs (paid for by Crown Brand) the kids,

. . . knew every player by sight and they seemed to know the rules. Frequently cries of "offside" or "illegal interference" would arise from the boyish throats . . . At frequent intervals, a few would start up "Hail, Hail, the Gang's All Here" [Harry's theme song] and with the speed of a snowball growing as it runs down a hill the song would spread until every red-faced youngster was taking part in the really pleasant though impromptu concert. And these — the writer thought — are the paying Toronto rugby fans of tomorrow.

Over the next four or five years Sports Club members were treated to samples of just about every sporting event that Toronto had to offer. It was at these gatherings that Harry Foster was happiest. He loved being in charge of things and he loved being the centre of attention. He was almost always in the crowd, mingling with the kids, contorting his face and making his eyes wobble to everyone's delight. He signed autographs by the hundreds and generally raced around trying to make the youngsters feel that they were not alone. According to one sports writer, he took more kids to the bathroom than any other person in Canada. "I just couldn't stand seeing them with their teeth chattering and looking as if they had to go," Red once confessed.

Certainly the kids felt at home when he was on hand. Harry and the kids were a perfect match. He was both a cheerful youngster and an amazingly shrewd business man.

Harry signs autographs at a Crown Brand Sports Club event in 1936. Through his work in radio broadcasts and promotions he became a celebrity among the youth of Ontario.

The kids saw in him a friendly, not-so-old, formerly successful athlete with a clean and exciting record. He lived and breathed sports and good sense with infectious enthusiasm. His claim that the Crown Brand Sports Club was the oldest and largest of its kind anywhere was well founded. He might also have claimed that his club members got the most benefits from the sponsors!

Another successful venture, tied to the Crown Brand Sports Club soon after its inception, was the annual Popular Mutt Contest staged each summer at Sunnyside Beach Park just west of the Exhibition grounds. This was a spin-off of another popular CNE event of the day, the Dog Swim Derbys, which had been started by Lou Marsh of *The Toronto Star*. Harry saw an opportunity to promote Corn

Syrup by capitalizing on the publicity already generated by the dog swims. His contest would offer poorer children who did not own the better breeds of dogs a chance to display their pets and have some fun. "Somehow this Mutt Contest caught the fancy of the press. We broke into the papers like Bee Hive never could or ever will," Harry wrote in 1938. Every member of the Club was entitled to enter his or her canine pet, and prizes were offered for the dog with the longest tail, most breeds, loudest bark, best tricks, biggest, smallest and so on. The dogs themselves created the fun when they failed to perform on cue, and they brought the Club and the sponsors a great deal of excellent publicity.

In the 1938 contest, staged at Sunnyside, over three hundred dogs were entered and nearly 10,000 people are reported to have watched the proceedings as the children paraded their animals onto Harry's Crown Brand stage. Harry, the Master of Ceremonies, convinced local dignitaries to assist with the judging and prize giving and in doing so gave the occasion increased stature. The dignitaries came partly because Harry was so persistent and partly because the program that Harry put together with the kids really was howling good fun.

At one contest, Harry's eye fell on a little boy in a wheel chair who held his dog on his lap throughout the show. The lad was not a contestant, but when the prizes were being handed out Harry went down into the audience and presented a new prize for the Best Behaved Dog! The boy, his parents and the crowd were thrilled. This added "touching moment" was typical of Harry's knack for doing the right thing at the right time. Chances are that the boy in the wheelchair became a Crown Brand user for life, but Harry's heart was in the right place from the beginning. The promotional side was the bonus.

The radio Sports Club, with its excursions to sporting events, and the Popular Mutt Contests, with their absence of snobbishness, were all tremendous successes. By the

A hearty crowd of Crown Brand Sports Club members cheers during a sporting event at the Canadian National Exhibition grounds.

'Red' Foster stands at the centre of attention in his sports car in a crowd of Six-Day cycling enthusiasts at the Canadian National Exhibition grounds' Princess Gate in 1935.

fourth anniversary of the Club in April, 1939, Harry had chalked up over five hundred radio broadcasts. For Harry, promoting the product was the means of promoting the best ideals of sport and team spirit and just plain fun. The sponsor still had to pay the bills, however, and the enthusiasm Harry could muster with the kids was nearly equalled by his own enthusiasm for Crown Brand Syrup. Club membership also gave the youthful listeners access to a prominent radio voice. The filing cabinets in his office were crammed with folders full of neatly ruled letters starting with "Dear Red . . ." or "Dear Uncle Red . . ." along with

carbon copies of Harry's conscientious replies. None of the benefits of Club membership, however, were better demonstrated than at the annual December Ice Carnivals at Maple Leaf Gardens.

These carnivals were true spectacles which became an institution with the younger set in Toronto at Christmas time. Harry made them bigger and better each year from 1935 through 1940. With fancy skating exhibitions, acrobatic clown acts, barrel jumping and an abundance of bands providing the music, Harry demonstrated his skill in knowing what children liked. There was always a short broom-

The cover of the program and songsheet that was handed out at the Crown Brand Sports Club Christmas Ice Carnival in 1939.

Gardens. Harry always began these games with an emotionally charged official face-off. On one occasion, "Ace" Bailey, the Maple Leaf legend whose career ended late in 1933 with an unfortunate cross-check from Eddie Shore, had the honours. On another occasion, Harry got Alfred Scadding, one of the Toronto men who was trapped in the famous Moose River Mine disaster of 1936, to drop the puck. These were all examples of Harry's genuine desire to honour people who had made contributions one way or another to Canadian life and, at the same time, to milk them for their publicity value.

The Red Foster Christmas shows also included a chari-

Children at the Christmas Ice Carnival could expect to be entertained by such antics as clowns in oversized cans of corn syrup.

ball game made up of local old-timers or policemen versus firemen. These gave the children opportunities to cheer heartily for one side or the other.

A not-too-serious hockey game was also a favourite item which allowed Harry (and the kids) to enjoy an association with the big names of the game. In 1939, for instance, Lionel Conacher's All Stars met King Clancy's Challengers and the resulting cheering contest rocked the table angle and Harry made sure that the best seats were reserved for handicapped children. This made it easy to attract the participation of scores of individual sports celebrities, the whole Toronto Maple Leaf Hockey Team on occasion, and political dignitaries from the mayor of Toronto to members of parliament. Most of all, however, the capacity crowds of well-behaved children enjoyed a tremendous amount of wholesome enjoyment. This fact was not lost on the Toronto Board of Education in 1936 when they registered their protest on behalf of a number of school principals who were besieged with notes and tel-ephone calls asking that their children might leave school early to attend the show.

This oversight in Harry's timing of his programs in 1935

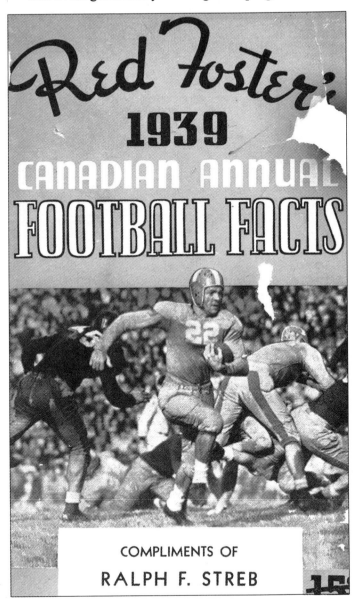

One of Harry Foster's earliest promotional projects was a CFL Canadian Annual Football Facts booklet.

Charlie Conacher and Harvey Jackson of the Toronto Maple Leafs help children into Red Foster's Christmas Ice Carnival at Maple Leaf Gardens in 1937.

Harry Foster brought wolves into the CBC in one of his forays into the world of public broadcasting.

bicycle races and many special and annual Toronto events including the Royal Winter Fair, the Horse Show, and the King's Plate horse race for a wide variety of sponsors.

The late 1930's must be seen as the great age of radio promotion and The Harry E. Foster Agencies was in the thick of it. Aside from the Crown Brand Sports Club activities, there were talent contests for Toronto area high school students who voted with bottle caps, and commercials for new radios which "threw in" Red Foster's *Canadian Annual Football Facts* booklet at no additional charge. There were free hockey tickets for guessing attendance figures at hockey games and, on one occasion, a grand prize of a hockey stick autographed by all of the Toronto Maple Leafs to the person who could guess the time of the first goal. Each entry was sent in on a shaving cream wrapper of course! *Marketing* Magazine is dotted with references to various agencies promoting products by means of gimmicks. Even the Canadian Broadcasting Corporation, the government owned network, got into the act with a ten minute broadcast with Harry as Master of Ceremonies built around a hockey scores guessing contest, sponsored by

and 1936 was corrected but it also led the Board of Education to reject his request for school board buses to transport the disabled children, so Harry had to devise other means. He usually broadcast a public appeal for cars or called upon his hockey friends from the Maple Leafs. In spite of this minor difficulty, the Carnivals continued to be the Christmas social highlight for Toronto youngsters. The kids won, Harry won, the performers won, and the Canada Starch Company increased its production capacity every year from 1935 through 1940.

Although the Sports Club activities took a great deal of planning and organization by Harry and his staff, he still found time to broadcast football and baseball games, some wrestling, swimming marathons at the CNE, the Six-Day

Harry used a variety of promotional tools to advertise his growing business, including coasters which looked like the labels from records.

Harry Foster's radio broadcasting van was a common sight at sporting events around Ontario.

Minty's toothpaste.

There is no record of any Foster involvement in the debate which raged throughout the 1930's on the merits and demerits of commercial broadcasting. The CBC had come into existence in 1936 under Mackenzie King's Liberal Government. The new public network struggled to compete with the other stations for good programming, without what was often termed "the nauseating overdoses of advertising." Some of its programs, on what was called the Dominion Network, still carried commercials, however, and Harry supplied some of these. He was firmly in the free enterprise commercial camp of course, and he was proving that commercial radio could indeed bring good Canadian programming to the public. The only indication of his stance on the subject is in an article cut from an issue of

Saturday Night magazine found among his papers and marked with his own bold red ink check marks. Noting the better American programming and the cool reception to CBC material, one underlined paragraph noted that,

. . . between the annual radio license fee and the school masterish attitude adopted by those in authority, the system of public service broadcasting has stood very little chance of winning the friendship of the Canadian listening public. Grudgingly and of necessity, we paid the piper but after doing so, showed our displeasure by refusing to listen to the tune!

There is no question that Harry always viewed the

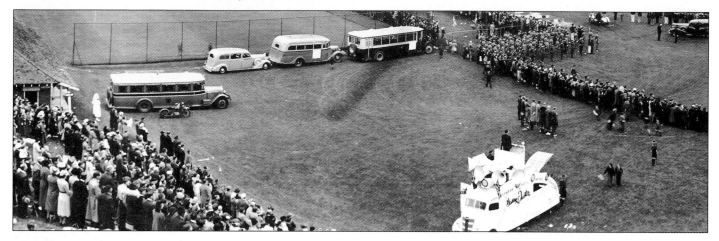

King George VI and Queen Elizabeth arrive at Riverdale Park in Toronto in front of an estimated crowd of 200,000. Harry Foster,

programming of Canada's public broadcaster with a somewhat jaundiced eye, perhaps foreseeing the agency for what it did in fact become (in his eyes anyway) – the chief judge and executioner of the competition.

While the Crown Brand Sports Club and some of Harry's special events were carried commercially by the CBC, Harry's other programs emanated from a variety of stations. One highly prominent program, which featured Harry exclusively from 1937 through 1944, was the regular newscast on CFRB beginning at five minutes before noon every weekday. This was a ten-minute program sponsored by Acme Farmers Dairy designed to catch mothers as they prepared lunch for their children coming home from school. Harry saw an opportunity to promote bottled milk at what seemed like an odd hour. Since prime time radio only began after 6:00 pm, morning radio had no apparent audience and car radio, of course, was unheard of. Harry therefore took a chance by straddling the noon hour when advertising rates were the cheapest. The gamble paid off and an audience at home and in barber shops was soon created. Unfortunately none of these broadcasts survive, but within a year the news had expanded to start at ten minutes before noon where it remains even to this day on CFRB. Typical of all his programs, which were dressed up with some sort of flair,

this popular newscast began musically with "The Parade of the Toy Soldiers."

There is certainly no doubt that Harry's broadcasting days in the late 1930's were busy ones. This already well established pattern of busyness was one which would continue for the rest of his life. The variety of activities also provided the background for the many anecdotes which he loved to recount years later. Early in 1936, for example, Harry was appointed the announcer for the first motion picture of a wrestling bout ever made in Canada. This "talkie" as films with audio were referred to, was staged at Maple Leaf Gardens and featured two local favourites, Londos and Zacharias, and Red's was the voice on the silver screen when it played briefly in Toronto. Unfortunately, neither the film nor Harry's film career survived!

On another occasion, a promotion almost cost him "an arm and a leg" when a hunter from Hudson's Bay brought two large timber wolves to Toronto to prove that wolves are really cowardly creatures which will not attack unless cornered. This was a promotion of *The Toronto Star* which paid for and reaped the publicity. Harry, seeing an opportunity for fun, invited the hunter and his wolves to his CBC studio for an interview. Although the animals wore chain collars, one of them nipped the hunter whose hand then

whose mobile studio van in the lower left, entertained the crowd for over two hours before the arrival of the monarchs.

dripped blood throughout the interview. Only a couple of brave souls went into the studio to watch the broadcast and Harry reported, "You should have seen the CBC officials and other onlookers scuttle for safety when the two wolves were brought out from the studio!"

Harry Foster took full advantage of the many opportunities that presented themselves in the late 1930's, and he created much of his own luck. Typical of his promotional mind set was the purchase of the first ever mobile studio and public address system. This was a gleaming white streamlined truck custom fitted onto a General Motors chassis. Here was a broadcasting studio filled with equipment and loudspeakers and featuring a fold-out platform at the back where the announcer could stand. It was reported to have cost Harry $14,000 (a large sum in those days) and was a sensational exhibit in itself when it made its appearance at the Canadian National Exhibition in August 1937. News broadcasts from the truck in front of curious CNE spectators were the first programs to issue forth and it was not long before his studio on wheels was crossing the province from event to event with its loudspeaker system and the ever cheerful Harry. The mobile studios (there would eventually be three of them) soon became a familiar sight at football games, and later at political rallies, outdoor church services

and the annual New Year's Eve parties at Toronto's City Hall.

Harry's sound system was also used when the King George VI and Queen Elizabeth visited Canada in May 1939 on their Royal Tour just before the outbreak of the Second World War. Enormous preparations were undertaken across the country, but nowhere more than in Toronto, the heart of English Canada. The city fairly oozed with patriotic fervour and genuine love for the monarchs. Record breaking crowds along the route of the Royal Tour had to be accommodated, and the largest of these gathered at Riverdale Park, just south of the Danforth viaduct, under the direction of Harry E. Foster himself. This area was a perfect natural amphitheatre for a crowd estimated at well above the 200,000 mark, the largest crowd ever gathered in a single spot anywhere in Canada up to that time. Fully one-half of this enormous throng was children, organized school by school. Students were bused or trained from outlying areas as far away as Owen Sound and Peterborough. Weeks of advance planning by schools and police included Harry and his gigantic sound system to help keep this huge army of children, without their parents, both orderly and in good spirits. Harry Foster was perfect for the job.

The park was virtually full two hours before the entry of

THE EVENING TELEGRAM, TORONTO, THURSDAY, F

"RED" FOSTER WEDS IN NEW YORK

Harry E. ("Red") Foster, of Toronto, well known | in New York on Tuesday. They are honeymooning as a one-time all-round athlete and as a radio sports | Sea Island, Georgia. Mr. Foster, who played foot announcer and advertising executive, and Miss Kathryn | for the Balmy Beach team, is the son of Mr. and M ("Jimmie") Taylor, daughter of Mr. and Mrs. Percy | D. H. Foster.

Harry Foster and Kathryn Taylor's 1939 wedding announcement in the Toronto Telegram.

the Royal entourage. Inevitably, they were late in arriving and Harry was forced to fill the time and keep the multitude of anxious children at ease. He handled this with characteristic ease by relating short anecdotes from the sports world, by rehearsing the national anthems, and by combining general chit chat with up-to-the-minute information on the progress of the Royal procession as it wound its way through the city. At last the mounted escort swept into view, followed by their Majesties in an open car. The cheers of the children swept across the park as the Royal Standard was raised. The bodyguard wheeled their horses into line and the King stepped from his car and mounted the platform to the chord for "God Save the King." This was the signal arranged in rehearsal an hour before for the entire crowd to join in the singing of the National Anthem. Before the royal car moved out towards the children, there was a very brief word of welcome and a short prayer. Just as the prayer was

announced, the crowd heard "Everything OK up there Pete?" as the frequency of the new police radios somehow crossed with those of the loudspeaker system!

The decade of the 1930's was an incredibly active one for Harry. He established himself as a broadcaster of sports, an advertiser, a promoter and as the "King of the Kids." His agency made recordings for special events and his loudspeaker systems were on the go much of the time. In spite of all the busyness, however, Harry maintained his contacts with his sporting friends, found time for a little horse riding of his own and for old-timer hockey and baseball games with the boys. There was not much time left for an active pursuit of romance, although he must have been considered one of Toronto's most impeccably dressed and most eligible bachelors. He certainly had a reputation as somewhat of an expert in the Charleston dance step and his sports car was a familiar sight in downtown Toronto. It was reported that the police were well aware his habit of always being in a hurry, especially when he sometimes parked his car on the sidewalk when spaces were unavailable!

Harry had met his one and only true love in the rowdy days of the late 1920's and he had had an on-again, off-again relationship with her throughout the 1930's. She was Kathryn "Jimmie" Taylor, a somewhat headstrong and independent-minded modelling beauty from the Beaches area, the daughter of film distributor and local sportsman Percy Taylor. On one occasion she wrecked Harry's sports car but no details of that incident have survived.

The couple finally decided to marry in January 1939 and they quietly slipped off to New York City for both wedding and honeymoon, much to the chagrin of the local press which was thus denied a big story. This was one ceremony which Harry did not consider a public event. The couple were back in Toronto within a week and took up residence on Edmund Avenue just two blocks from the old Foster family home on Oaklands Avenue. Harry's domestic routines certainly changed dramatically after his marriage but, with the war clouds growing darker in Europe throughout 1939, everyone's routines were on the brink of change.

Chapter Six
On the Home Front

From the mid 1930's, it was obvious to almost everyone that a serious conflict in Europe was brewing. The tensions overseas, created mainly by the rise of Adolf Hitler, were a factor in the demand for regular radio newscasts as peace-loving Canadians sought to know more about a world which seemed to be moving closer to disaster with each passing month. Domestic excitement, such as the birth of the Dionne Quints in 1934 and the world-wide coverage of the dramatic Moose River Mine disaster in 1936 in Nova Scotia, also encouraged people to turn regularly to their radios.

When World War Two began in September 1939, it did not come as much of a surprise anywhere. Officially, the war came to Canada on the 10th of that month, with a declaration from England by King George VI that was heard simultaneously across the nation. A War Measures Act, giving the government wide powers to protect Canadian security followed quickly on the heels of the declaration. For the first eight months of the war, however, the government held to its policy of limited war preparedness. The months that followed the declaration were known everywhere as the "phony war." Because nothing seemed to happen, it encouraged both a degree of uncertainty and a certain complacency. Neither Canadian industry, still hurting from the effects of the Great Depression, nor the armed services were prepared for serious warfare. Except for some early army recruiting, the logical thing for most people to do was to carry on with their lives.

Harry Foster was never complacent about the war, but carrying on as before seemed entirely appropriate in late 1939. The regular Crown Brand Sports Club radio programs continued, along with the ten-to-twelve news on CFRB. The sound trucks were busy at special events, and a new weekly program called "Sports Parade with Harry Foster" had begun in July on the CBC network. Play-by-play commentating on football games including the Grey Cup final consumed his broadcasting energies that autumn and he set the exhaustive plans for his fifth annual Crown Brand Ice Carnival into motion. Having outgrown his MacLean Building quarters on Dundas Street, Harry had begun negotiations with the King Edward Hotel for new studio quarters. On top of all of this, a new house, his new wife, and new domestic responsibilities kept Harry busier than ever.

Verbally, Harry supported the rush for voluntary enlistment in the army, but the thought of joining up never crossed his mind, even though Ted Reeve and Jimmy Keith (his old pals from football days) and First World War veteran Conn Smythe of Maple Leaf hockey fame, were making plans to go overseas. Harry was still an eligible thirty-five year old, but bad ankles and knees, combined with what he saw as his continuing obligation to help look after his brother Jackie, destined Red for the home front.

Early in 1940, the Walter M. Lowney Company, the makers of the "Oh Henry!"® chocolate bar, entered the Foster picture. Like the Canada Starch Company, Lowneys saw the benefits of exploiting the children's market. At the same time, they wanted to be seen doing useful community service. They approached Harry and the "King of the Kids" saw another promotional opportunity. His idea of a Safety Club for children quickly won the Lowney Company's approval. Aside from Harry's own love of children and his credentials as a promoter, one only has to read the newspapers of the day to understand the need for such a club.

In 1939 alone, more than ninety children between the ages of five and fourteen were killed in automobile accidents in Ontario, along with more than 2,000 injured. North America was only slowly getting used to its love affair with fast cars on roads that were clearly unsafe by today's standards. There were few safety regulations for vehicles, and children, uneducated in safety principles, were paying a heavy price. The need to do something about the tragedy was real, and a private commercial initiative was welcomed by parents, governments and the Foster Agencies alike.

A new radio club took to the airwaves in March of 1940. This one was designed not to conflict with the Crown Brand Sports Club which had been on the air since 1935, but it would clearly operate along the same lines. The program was launched with a fanfare of entertainment at a banquet at the King Edward Hotel in true Foster style. The Mayor of Toronto and leaders of various civic groups were invited, as was the Police Chief, the Fire Chief, the Ontario Motor League and the President of the Lowney Company. Everyone spoke in support of the idea and Harry, of course, had the last word.

The Lowney's Young Canada Club, as it was called, would air continuously twice a week for just over five years. Their adopted motto "Safety First and Play the Game" had a decided Foster ring to it! There would be serialized stories and dramatized safety incidents. Boys and girls would enrol (with a chocolate bar wrapper) and receive buttons and certificates for learning the rules of the road. It was intended that individual communities would sponsor a Safety Club, with radio support from Toronto, to make children more safety conscious. The Club met with considerable success in this aspect during the war period. Accident statistics in communities which launched such programs did improve and one lasting benefit, which is still in evidence in Ontario, is the school safety patrol system which Harry's Young Canada Club played a significant role in establishing.

The Lowney's Young Canada Club membership card.

Along with the radio program, Harry added a road show called Lowney's Young Canada Caravan. This travelling safety circus visited many communities in Ontario and Quebec in 1940 with Saturday morning entertainment of all sorts to help hammer home the safety messages. Harry believed that the best way to make an impact was to employ local children and adults almost exclusively in each town that the caravan visited. Children would be coached to demonstrate the wrong way and the right way of riding bicycles, roller skating and even skipping rope. Some bigger boys would be conscripted to carry Department of Highway signs and the fire department would demonstrate the proper handling of accident victims. The most dramatic part of the show was a parade of ninety or more local children representing the province's fatalities of the previous year. This in itself had impact. After the demonstrations, the children would all be treated to a movie at the local theatre. It was all pure promotion for chocolate bars, but the messages did get through with marked effect. The kids won, Lowney's won and Harry Foster won again.

As the Lowney's programs took off in popularity and the Safety Circuses began to filter into the province with their important messages, the time came for Harry's long awaited move to new business quarters in the King Edward

In a Lowney's Young Canada Club Safety Parade, children hold signs extolling the virtues of playing safely.

Hotel. This move was clearly a result of the need for more studio space due to the increased amount of radio production. In spite of Harry's popularity as an upstanding broadcaster, his reputation preceded him and he literally had to talk his way into the building with negotiations that had been in progress for almost a year. The manager of the hotel well remembered the antics of the football gang a decade earlier and still harboured a fear for his furnishings! Harry posted a bond for his offices on the mezzanine floor and in the beginning paid for his space in advance. Business is business, however, and soon every time Foster used the line "... brought to you from the King Edward Hotel ..." on any broadcast, he got a reduction in rent.

The first Harry E. Foster Agencies studio and offices opened with a black-tie ceremony in May, 1940. People were welcomed to watch a program in progress, or to listen as the broadcasts of various items were piped down to the main lobby — another Foster first. A teletype machine brought in a wider news network, and there were direct wire communications with every other broadcasting station in Toronto, so that Harry could now do his programs without ever leaving his studio. This was the continuation of the agency cementing its foundations in broadcasting. Over the course of the war years the studios themselves expanded, eventually consuming most of the King Edward's mezzanine floor.

The move to the King Edward Hotel had come at precisely the right time and was a classic example of Harry's ability to create his own luck. In the spring of 1940, the whole character of the war changed. Had Harry delayed his move, economic changes everywhere might have made it impossible. The Battle of Britain, the fall of France and the evacuation from Dunkirk shattered what was left of the notion of a "phony war." The real war had begun and Canada began its rapid gearing up to meet the challenge. Canadian factories began humming again, unemployment vanished almost overnight, and some consumer goods like chocolate, sugar and gasoline became less available. A deflated economy was reinflating rapidly.

The Harry Foster Agencies adapted to these changes with remarkable ease. The Lowney's Caravan soon shifted away from children's safety to travelling entertainment for

The Lowney's Young Canada Club Safety Circus stage, circa 1940, was the centrepiece of a show which travelled to communities around Ontario.

praise on the effort, declaring that:

> *Any one less determined would have been disheartened by the red tape, the buck passing and the spineless attitude of certain authorities. But Mr. Foster never lost heart. His enthusiasm rose supreme.... We feel it is but fair to call attention to the*

Harry held a Popular Mutt Contest in August 1940 to assist British children displaced by the war.

indefatigable efforts of Mr. Foster who has rapidly become one of the most useful citizens in Toronto.

The Toronto Telegram, on the other hand, was less complimentary.

> *... without detracting in any way from the reputation of Red Foster in his chosen line or reflecting upon the patriotism of his purpose ... it must be stated that it [the blackout] is to be regarded as a waste of money and a washout .... As a publicity stunt ... the blackout could only compel the thought that committees are as putty in the hands of a good salesman.*

Whether the exercise was really a useful one or merely a stunt depends upon one's point of view. Despite the difference of opinion it did get everybody's attention; it did bring the war in Europe a bit closer to everyone's mind and the sales of bonds the day after the blackout set a new record, bringing in over $14 million.

More spectacular headlines, however, came from the giant rallies at Maple Leaf Gardens that were masterminded by Harry for the Third through the Seventh War

Loan Campaigns. Harry was the Master of Ceremonies in each of these, and crowds above 17,000 were regularly in attendance. The shows were similar in nature to the Ice Carnivals, but on these occasions it was mostly an adult crowd, and there was always one featured guest artist. The guests on several occasions included the British singing star Gracie Fields, the American popular radio team of Fibber McGee and Molly, and the American Republican politician Wendell Wilkie. In 1942, the Dionne Quints were the big drawing card; under Harry's direction, they stole the show. Their stay at the King Edward Hotel was Harry's engineering as well. Maple Leaf Gardens was always decked in flags and the stage was always centred below a giant portrait of King George VI. Regular fare included military pageantry and displays from the armed services, recorded clips of Churchill's speeches, short descriptions of battles by service men, Red Cross messages and, of course, speeches about the need to buy bonds.

Harry was in his element with these wartime extravaganzas. His experience in piecing together the dozens of parts that constituted each rally, and his proficiency behind the microphone in keeping the action flowing for two hours and more, made each show a masterpiece of organized entertainment. In a manner that was virtually patented by

As the war effort on the home front began in earnest, Harry worked to generate revenue for the government through victory rallies such as this one held at Maple Leaf Gardens in 1942. The shows combined entertainment featuring famous stars like Gracie Fields with an appeal for money to help the war effort.

The Harry E. Foster Agencies' sound trucks were converted into Red Cross vehicles during the war.

this time, he was able to make the thousands of people who attended believe that their presence (and subsequent purchase of Victory Bonds) was indeed a crucial part of the war effort. In short, Harry tried to ensure that they got good value for their time and money. From the script of the Second Victory Loan Program comes this sample of showmanship:

> *Girl drives up the centre aisle on motorcycle . . .*
> *Foster gets the message from her . . . [excited voice]*
> *"Ladies and gentlemen, I have just received a most*
> *important telegram! Our guest star of the evening is*
> *about to make her entrance! Here she comes now*

> *— Miss Gracie Fields!" Trumpeters' fanfare accompanies applause.*

There is no doubt from attendance figures and bond sales that the shows were successful. Eventually, criticism was aimed at the high cost of bringing Hollywood stars to the big cities to tell Canadians to buy bonds. Harry and many other promoters argued that without the high priced talent, people would not listen to the sales message. Patriotism simply needed to be prodded. One critical editorial finally surrendered on the issue by noting that:

Most laymen think there's a good deal of hokum in an ad man's estimate of his own worth. But it must be admitted that if the Victory Loan technique is wrong on this point, so is the whole sales practice of North American business. We rely on ballyhoo to sell everything from lollipops to luxury liners.

If Harry Foster had any critics during the war years, they would have accused him of being one of the "kings of ballyhoo," a promoter pure and simple with a sharp eye on making money. Everything Harry did, he did with flair, polish and tremendous enthusiasm, and he always relished his role which put him front and centre. Harry did make money, but not on the Victory Loan campaigns; there were too many regulations governing them. There is no question, however, about Harry's personal patriotic desire to do what he could for the home front war effort. Since he could not go overseas himself, he believed that his was an equally important contribution.

Opportunities to promote patriotism were nowhere more frequent than on the air in his daily CFRB newscasts. Telling the stories of events on the front lines as they flowed from the wire services became regular fare throughout the war period. In the early years of the war, getting the best stories was often difficult because of wartime censorship regulations and the fact that the news from the front was often not very good.

On one dramatic occasion, Harry was saved from the embarrassment of being too enthusiastic. The day after the famous Dieppe Raid in August, 1942, Harry received a recording from an American journalist of the actual daylight raid which sounded as if a great Canadian victory was unfolding. Fortunately (or unfortunately), the journalist did not pronounce the word "Saskatchewan" properly and since The South Saskatchewan Regiment figured prominently in the attack, the word appeared many times. The recording itself was not on tape but on the standard aluminium based acetate disk which looked somewhat like one of the old 78 rpm plastic records. The grooves were cut in the studio with a sapphire needle and once grooved, they could not be changed or patched over.

However eager Harry was to air the report with its apparent good news, he felt that it could not be used in its original state. He immediately called Gordon Sinclair, his friend and roving reporter, who was out of work at the time, to come over to the studio to fix the problem. Sinclair said he could do a better piece himself, but before he had his piece ready, the wire services were indicating that the raid was not a glorious victory but a disaster of the first order. Sinclair did create the new story for Harry (with the facts adjusted correctly) in what would be the first of the series of programs that would ultimately be called "Let's Be Personal." These began on a regular basis in August of 1944 and would become an institution for over forty years on CFRB.

Out of that incident, the seed for another idea was planted which would also blossom in 1944. This was Harry's "Command Performance" program, a radio drama featuring the exploits of the winners of the Victoria Cross. The first two programs that Harry produced in fact were based on Sinclair's scripts and dealt with Lieutenant Colonel Charles Merritt of the South Saskatchewan Regiment and Reverend John Foote, the padre who had volunteered to stay with the Dieppe prisoners.

Radio continued to be the medium where Harry got the most exposure as "a voice" on the airwaves. His personality shone brightest, however, in the many special events which came his way. Although the Victory Loan campaigns were the most frequent of these, one very special opportunity to be front and centre came in 1943. Harry Foster's continued enthusiasm to be part of the drive for victory and his connections with the radio world made him the logical choice to be the broadcaster for the multiple christening of five Victory Ships at Superior, Wisconsin, in May of that year. This was to be no ordinary boat launching. The Dionne Quints, who had been in Toronto under Harry's care at the King Edward Hotel less than a year before, were to be the guests of honour. The Walter Butler Shipyards were anxious to highlight Superior's role in the working world's contribution to the massive American defence and home front effort of the war. Five vessels had been prepared for the May launching. The attendance of the Dionnes was considered by the Wisconsin authorities to be the frosting on the occasion.

In early May, Harry Foster headed for North Bay, where the whole Dionne family was to board a special train for the journey to the head of Lake Superior. This was to be the first time the nine-year-old quints would travel outside Ontario; as wards of the Province, a special bill had to be passed by the Ontario Legislature to permit their leaving. On Thursday, May 6, two sleeping cars pulled by a CN locomotive chugged out of North Bay, the first train ride the Quints had ever experienced. The lead car contained the Dionne family and the family's long time medical advisor, Dr. Allan Dafoe. Harry, his secretary, and a bevy of dignitaries and security people rode in the second car. Harry had arranged that most of their food would travel with them and, on the doctor's advice, the drinking water from the Dionne farm as well. This would prevent any possible upset to the Quints' digestive systems. Harry also guarded a container of christening water from the Niagara River sent to him by the mayors of Niagara Falls, Ontario and Niagara Falls, New York, as a symbol of the international effort to win the war.

In the days prior to their arrival in Superior, the Quints' entire life story was told and retold in the local papers. Even the Crown Brand-St. Lawrence Starch corn syrup squabble had been reviewed. Everybody in Wisconsin seemed to want a glimpse of the famous children. This was evident from the moment of their arrival on Saturday. A spectacular celebration had been organized. White, red and blue streamers were everywhere, a naval marching band greeted the train on its arrival, and the governor invited everyone to a mammoth state luncheon. Special bleachers had been constructed at every safe vantage point along the docks. Every seat was sold for Sunday's launchings, but the crowds were much in evidence even on Saturday afternoon when the Dionne children were treated to their first ever motorboat ride around the site.

Sunday began with a mass for the Quints delivered by the Bishop of Superior. This was followed with photo opportunities for the throngs of media. Harry's job was not only to broadcast the events but also to engineer the various appearances of the Quints and to try to hold the media at bay as best he could. He also conferred with the networks and prepared the hook-ups for the broadcast before the launching.

Harry was the only broadcaster to actually interview the Quints on the platform in front of the hundreds of workers and dignitaries. Since Harry's abilities in French were severely limited, and since the girls did not speak English with any fluency, the words broadcast that day were ones which had all been carefully rehearsed during the train journey. Harry's biggest fear was mixing up the names of the girls, because even he couldn't tell them apart! Fortunately, his secretary saved the day just before the pre-launch ceremonies with little name tags for their lapels. An even more delicate problem was the planned singing of "God Bless America," which the Quints of course did not know. When the time came for the anthem, Harry engineered the shipbuilder's daughters in behind the celebrities, and they rendered the appropriate verses. The radio listeners never knew the difference.

The actual launchings, one each by Annette, Cecile, Emile, Marie and Yvonne, were accomplished in the space of two hours and twenty minutes, a record never equalled for such things. Each of the Quints smashed her tethered pint-sized bottle of Niagara River water perfectly against each hull as it slipped sideways down its ramp. In the recording that was made of the broadcast, the cheering of the crowds can still be heard each time as each freighter hit the water.

Harry Foster could be justly proud of the whole occasion. He had organized yet another event in the aid of the total war effort, this time with a distinct international flavour. His voice had been heard across North America, and was soon carried to England. As expected, the Quints had won the hearts of the Americans. As the train left that Sunday night for the trip back to North Bay and as the newly christened ships began their journeys to England, Harry and everyone else could certainly rest assured that five more nails had been hammered into Hitler's coffin.

As promotional spectacles, the Victory Loan rallies and the trip to Superior, Wisconsin, belong in the category of special events. What was continuous and more far reaching was the creation and broadcasting of Canadian programming. During the war years there was no more important business than promoting patriotism, and both the Crown Brand Sports Club and the Lowney's Safety Club were tremendous vehicles for doing just that. The interviews that had been central to Harry's Sports Club broadcasts changed with the circumstances and emphasized the deeds of athletes now in the armed services. Harry always pointed out to his listeners that the teamwork they had formerly exhibited on the playing fields at home was now standing them in good stead on the battlefields. Stories about prominent athletes would be used to demonstrate the value of athletics, and Harry would regularly proclaim that such stories would "convince the enemies of freedom that Canada's heritage on the playing field [was] a right that we [would] fight to defend."

By early 1944, the Crown Brand Sports Club had run its course. After nine years of keeping its audiences up to date in the sports world, as well as amused with Harry's remarkably accurate predictions of the outcomes of various sporting contests, the sponsors ended their long and successful promotion. The cost of maintaining Harry and all of the free benefits that had gone along with the club were too much for the wartime austerity of the Canada Starch Company.

The Lowney's Young Canada Club would continue until 1948; with its safety messages and words of patriotic encouragement, it thrived. During the war years, Harry made his listeners feel as though they were playing an important part in bringing the struggle to a successful conclusion. "Taking extra care. . . and avoiding unneces-

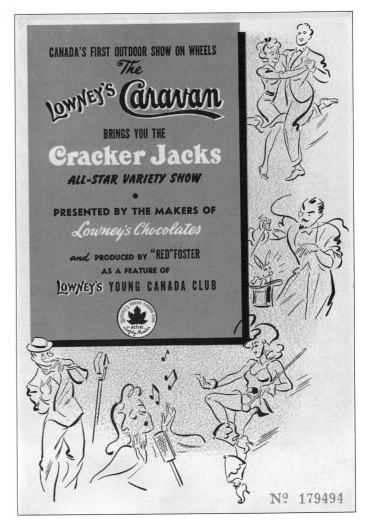

During the war, Lowney's Young Canada Club began presenting variety shows for troops stationed throughout Ontario, such as the one advertised on the cover of this program.

sary chances. . . may seem to some like a very small way of helping Canada's war effort," Harry often told his young listeners, "But it isn't! If . . . by taking extra care . . . you can avoid an unnecessary accident, you may be saving just that little bit of time or material that might be enough to turn the balance in an all-out struggle with the enemy. So let's all think safety and promote safety every minute."

Harry introduces the Dionne Quintuplets to a crowd at Superior, Wisconsin. The Quints had been invited as honoured guests to launch five freighters that were destined for service in the North Atlantic.

If safety consciousness among children was a more long term benefit, the short term advantage of belonging to the Young Canada Club was the on-air recognition the children got, and the featured serials that were attached to each program. Harry inaugurated Honour Certificates not only for safety work, but, "for anything outstanding done by any boy or girl in assisting or furthering Canada's war effort against the enemy of mankind." These certificates were even signed by the president of the Lowney Company. Names were read over the air of dozens of children from all across the country who did such things as collecting old newspapers, bottles, milkweed pods (for experiments in parachute construction and the stuffing for mattresses) and scrap metal.

Harry always heaped extra praise on special contributors such as the disabled girl from Winnipeg who, at twelve years of age, had just completed her 49th pair of knitted socks, or the boy from Welland, Ontario, who saved a baby from drowning in the Welland Canal. School, church and other specific groups were named when they undertook projects to raise money to buy War Savings Stamps and Certificates. What Harry always recognized over the airwaves was not the amounts raised, but the effort involved. Everyone on the home front was being encouraged to do his or her share, and every little bit helped both to win the war and to get them their regular doses of radio listening pleasure.

Interestingly, Dominic Morabito, the boy from Welland

Harry and one of the Dionne Quintuplets have some fun at the King Edward Hotel in Toronto.

who saved the life of the baby, still remembers the incident vividly. The baby was being wheeled along the canal bank in a buggy on a cold March day by an older brother who slipped and lost control. Buggy and baby both tumbled down the icy bank and the baby fell out, landing in the water but miraculously, on top of its blanket. Dominic ripped off his suit jacked and dove in. The next thing he remembers, he was back on the bank shivering with the infant. Both youngsters grew up in Welland, both worked at the Atlas Steel Company, and both remain good friends to this day. Harry picked up the story from the newspaper wire services and used it to make a point about bravery.

The talk and promotional portion of the shows was always followed by the featured presentation which Harry introduced himself with his typical flair and enthusiasm. Perhaps the most successful of these began in 1943 with the dramatized exploits of the Royal Canadian Mounted Police in the program "Men in Scarlet." The Mounties always got their man in this series which extended eventually to 434 separate episodes. Equally dramatic were the stories on "Command Performance" sponsored by Supertest Petroleum in 1944 and 1945, and the popular adaptations of

Canadian author Frank L. Packard's detective novels "The Adventures of Jimmy Dale," paid for by Dr. Jackson's "Munchies" breakfast cereal. "Jimmy Dale" and "Command Performance" only lasted until the end of the war, but the pattern of a patriotic chat followed by an exciting chapter of a radio drama enthused a whole generation and sold the products associated with it as well.

In many ways, the episodes in the "Jimmy Dale" and the "Men in Scarlet" series reflected Harry's own ever optimistic frame of mind as those noble myths of the age, that crime never pays, evil is always punished and goodness receives its just reward. The same might even be said of the "Command Performance" programs, where the evil portrayed was the Fascist cause and the awards to the Victoria Cross winners were the British Empire's highest honour.

What Red Foster did during the war years was to establish himself and his agency as Canadian leaders in the field of wholesome promotion and broadcasting. He had gathered around himself a staff of very creative and supportive people. They could back up any client's promotion with what was considered exciting programming which satisfied the escapist urges of Canadian radio audiences at that particular time. As a key personality in the Victory Bond drives and other special events, Harry had also become a leader on the home front, particularly in the Toronto area.

The credentials Harry had built would provide the base for the next logical step in his career — the establishment of a full-fledged advertising agency early in 1944. Here he could deal directly with his clients and expand the radio arm of a business that already had fifteen-year-old roots. Proving his solvency by scraping up all of his available cash and putting a mortgage on his sound trucks and radio equipment, he did break into the advertising business with a franchise which granted him formal recognition in May, 1944. The Harry E. Foster Agencies Limited became Harry E. Foster Advertising Limited. This was the big step. Once admitted to that inner circle of recognized advertising agencies, Harry would not leave it for another thirty years.

Chapter Seven
Building the Business

Gaining recognition from the various business groups that regulated the advertising industry was not an easy step for Harry Foster. Without official recognition, no freelance agency could deal directly with or collect commissions from the clients it hoped to serve. The regulators, called the Canadian Daily Newspaper Association, were dominated, as their name suggests, by newspaper interests. These newspapers disliked competition and had traditionally feared that radio broadcasting would destroy everything from the recording industry to reading itself. They were very cautious about letting a mere broadcaster with a flamboyant reputation into what was then a very conservative and virtually closed shop.

As a tireless worker in the war effort with a proven ability to affect the lives of Canadians across the country through radio, however, Harry had established his credentials and had earned the opportunity. His franchise, when granted, was the first addition to that association in over seven years. Harry was welcomed into the group by Jack MacLaren, the founder of Canada's largest agency at the time. In 1944, MacLaren predicted that Red would be the president of one of Canada's largest advertising agencies someday. Harry never doubted this and in the back of his mind for the next 25 years was his ambition to be number one on the list.

The first thing Harry had to do, in June 1944, was to abandon his ten-to-twelve news broadcast on CFRB because the sponsor, Acme Farmers Dairy, was a client of Cockfield, Brown, another leading agency. This would make Cockfield, Brown a competitor of the new Foster Agency. Leaving the news microphone was not a difficult step for Harry, however, because official enfranchisement of his agency had set him on the path toward new opportunities and challenges which would only be hampered by a regular time commitment. The announcing job incidentally went to Gordon Sinclair who maintained that time spot for a generation. That was the only major change in the early months of the franchise; the other regular programs continued uninterrupted. The broadcasting base which Harry had built, continued to grow after the war in the decade that would be labelled the Golden Age of Radio. This was a memorable era in Canadian history when children and adults alike were glued to their radio sets as avidly as today's generation watches television. Harry would always be proud of the contribution his agency made to that Golden Age and he would often say that Harry E. Foster Advertising Limited was a business that radio built.

The programming which issued from Harry Foster's studios was typical of what other full-time radio stations were airing during the Golden Age. While Canadians could get their fill of American programs such as "The Lone Ranger" and "The Shadow," an enormous amount of Canadian talent was nurtured between 1944 and 1954 for a host of radio shows and, in this, Harry certainly did his part. He contracted only Canadian writers, announcers, actors and musicians and he was a strong influence in the encouragement of such future stars as Duke Ellington, Bert Niosi, Lorne Greene, John Drainie and Paul Sherman. Most of these personalities were simply looking for work when Harry took them on for various assignments.

During these years, Harry organized the largest version of a Canadian broadcasting transcription service outside of

Gordon Forsyth, an employee of Foster Advertising, sits in the recording booth at the company's offices in the King Edward Hotel. The technician in the foreground is using equipment to cut acetate disks for recording (circa 1944-1945).

the CBC. These transcriptions were recordings cut into the large aluminium-based acetate disks that contained the program and the sponsors' messages. These were then mailed to private stations across the country. In the programs that flowed from his agency, Harry's love for Canada and for Canadian youth in particular was always evident and the heroes in his programs were all rooted in Canadian history. This was certainly to be expected from a man who had been behind a microphone himself for well over a decade. Golden Age radio was certainly an escape for all

ages of people from the humdrum of everyday living and Harry had always attempted to fill the gaps with wholesome material. By today's standards, it was painfully innocent in moral tone and the language employed was as proper as Harry's suits. Now that Harry was on the production side of radio, the medium itself would become much more than fun for kids.

To Harry Foster, radio was now a combination of many things. First, it was drama. In "Men In Scarlet," which ran for six years with Lowney's Chocolate as the sponsor, the

Mounties criss-crossed Canada's frozen north maintaining law and order. The RCMP was much more generous with its back files in those days and Harry's clever script writers could take any basic police story and serialize it into an action-packed fifteen minutes. The writers always maintained the facts at the heart of the story but they did embellish the plots with fictitious dialogue and a repertoire of sound effects. That was the nature of radio drama. It was also made memorable by the voice of a young John Drainie who played the role of the hero, Sergeant North. Harry was very proud when this program won the broadcasting industry's Beaver Award in 1945 for best commercial children's radio program.

In "The Adventures of Jimmy Dale," a four-year run sponsored by Dr. Jackson's "Munchies" breakfast cereal, justice always won out and the bad guys never prospered. Starring in the role of the bad guy opposite Jimmy Dale was Lorne Greene, a young actor who had just left the CBC

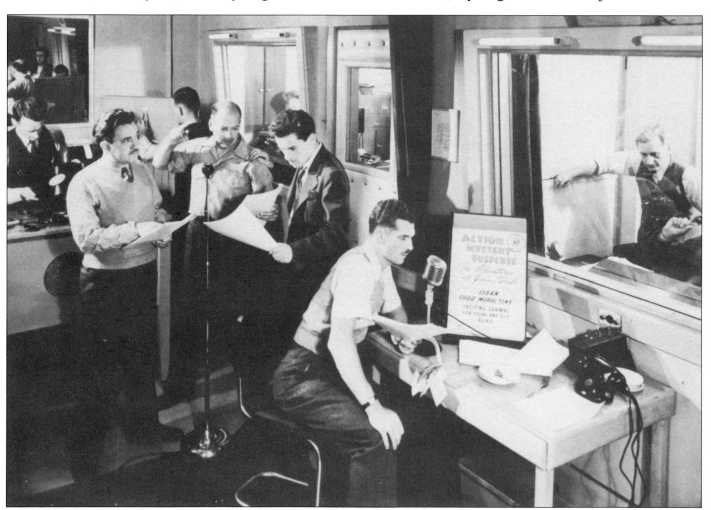

Foster employees record an episode of "The Adventures of Jimmy Dale," a popular radio serial during the 1940's.

For many years during the 1940s, Harry hosted the Saturday morning quiz show for high school students called "What's the Answer?" The show was held at Simpson's Arcadian Court and broadcast live on the radio.

newscasting department where, during the war, he had established his voice in the minds of Canadians as the "Voice of Doom." Greene was on the hunt for stage jobs and his sonorous tones would be heard in a number of radio roles before his stage career blossomed. Harry secured him for his programs at a lofty nine dollars per chilling episode!

The demise of the show in April, 1945, had nothing to do with Lorne Greene or the popularity of the program. The original Dr. Jackson, head of Dr. Jackson's Foods Limited, died and the company reorganized without Jimmy Dale. Harry loved to tell the story privately of that particular juncture. He had just taken a box of Dr. Jackson's pie crust mix home to test in his own kitchen. When he opened the box, a fat moth flew out; as it fluttered around the light bulb,

Harry received word that Dr. Jackson had passed away. Seeing humour in a sad piece of news, he recalled the moment as a drama on two fronts

Radio was also good music. Harry obtained the services of Sir Ernest MacMillan and the Toronto Symphony on behalf of Simpson's Department Store, and Paul Sherman for the Northern Electric Company. Their weekly pop concerts were a delight both to radio listeners and to live audiences alike. In fact, "The Northern Electric Hour" won the coveted LaFleche Trophy for the best commercial program both in 1946 and in 1947.

Radio was also entertainment. Harry himself was the master of ceremonies for "What's The Answer?" an hour of music and quiz which packed Simpson's Arcadian Court with high school students every Saturday morning for seven years, although Harry was not always behind the microphone. The good music and the entertainment aspects of radio were combined in the program "Command Performance" sponsored by Supertest Petroleum. This series was created originally to bolster the Victory Loan campaigns of 1944 and 1945. The shows were free and were staged at Massey Hall under Harry's direction.

They began with musical numbers by the Supertest Concert Orchestra and the Toronto Mendelssohn Choir under Sir Ernest MacMillan's baton. The musical portion was then followed with plugs for Victory Bonds and then the radio drama feature, a story of a particular Victoria Cross winner. It is hard for modern readers to contemplate a live audience sitting through a dramatic reading accompanied only by sound effects but here too Harry employed Lorne Greene as the narrator and it was the combination of

A masked Jimmy Dale character promotes breakfast cereal between solving mysteries in the popular radio series produced by Harry Foster's agency.

Greene's tremendous voice and the ability of the audiences of the era to imagine the action that made the series such a success.

Naturally enough, radio to Harry was also sports. Since the MacLaren Agency had hockey broadcasting tied up, Harry's attention became focused on football and Harry must get the credit for turning the Grey Cup into Canada's greatest sporting classic in the post-war years. As well as the regularly scheduled CFL games and the program called "Grey Cup Cavalcade," the Grey Cup Dinners and the Grey

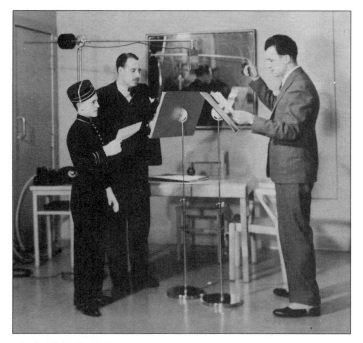

Harry Foster works in the studio with actors in the production of the commercial "Call for Phillip Morris" for the cigarette manufacturer.

Cup Parade before the final itself were all big items on the Foster Fall broadcasting schedule. In the years after the war, the annual Grey Cup games were brought to Canadians on radio from coast to coast with commercials through a network of as many as 75 private stations organized by Harry himself. In the early 1950's, when TV joined radio, Harry created an "agency-within-an-agency" group of a half dozen TV and radio experts who were busy full time with the organizational aspects of the autumn coverage.

Harry saw the Grey Cup east-west final and all the festivities associated with it as something uniquely Canadian and he promoted this with vigour. Believing that it was the meeting, greeting and good-natured fun that was most important at Grey Cup time, he reflected a gentler (and perhaps naive) era which sustained values quite different from our own. "It is the heartwarming sportsmanship and good fellowship [that] overrides partisan feelings," he told a Rotary luncheon in 1954. "Canadians from Atlantic to Pacific come closer together amid the glow of genuine warmth that seems to radiate at Grey Cup time." Harry Foster and the generation he represented believed these

Harry stands amid a pile of box top returns from a promotional advertising offer.

things with a passion. There is no doubt that he saw sports (and particularly football) as something that linked the country in a positive way; promoting this by means of radio and television was a responsibility which Harry took very seriously.

Above all, however, radio to Harry Foster was merchandising. He could convince advertisers that sponsoring his programs was the best way to promote their public image and to increase their visibility. The Crown Brand Sports Club was long remembered as one of the most spectacular merchandising efforts in Canadian advertising history and, in the period after 1945, that approach by the Foster Advertising Agency was not likely to change. In the Crown Brand days, Harry had developed an unerring sense of what would appeal to whom, and his use of radio as a merchandising tool was certainly the cornerstone of his early success. Exposure of a product on the airwaves brought results; combined with Harry's fondness for employing labels, coupons, box tops and prizes, the sales curves for his clients always seemed to move upwards.

One interesting illustration of the extent to which Harry could exploit radio as a promotional tool was shown by a busy week he spent with the Jimmy Dale character early in 1944. Harry took the masked radio personality to London, Ontario, to encourage the sale of both War Savings Stamps and Dr. Jackson's Roman Meal cereal at the same time. With Jimmy Dale in costume, they visited every school in the city delivering patriotic speeches. Harry then had Jimmy Dale walking around the city in ordinary street clothes and anyone who spotted him was rewarded with a pair of War Savings Stamps. Needless to say, since Dale's radio face was unknown, hundreds of males in London were accosted during the week! The radio hero and Red also called upon dozens of housewives and when they could produce a box of Roman Meal, they received four Savings Stamps.

The promotion ended with a rally at a local theatre on Saturday morning which actually had to be repeated in the afternoon to accommodate the crowds of children. Whether

The production crew prepares for the broadcast of the first Canadian television program. Because of a lack of Canadian facilities, Foster Advertising had to produce the show in Buffalo and broadcast live to Toronto.

the main purpose of the exercise was fun for the kids, or increased sales of the product, or more trade in Victory Stamps, or even more exposure for the "Jimmy Dale" program is hard to determine; they all went hand in hand from Harry's point of view.

In organizing sponsors' messages and in directing the radio programs themselves both on stage and in the studio, Harry became a master of detail. Indeed he had to be. There were dozens of parts to any given show and while he had capable people performing the varied duties, Harry was never far behind in making sure that every angle was covered. He was the type of person who would have two

projectors ready to screen a film, one to show it and the second to swing into action if the first broke down. And what came across the air was also always carefully screened. If it wasn't, he would certainly hear about it from his sponsors. The young Don Harron, a radio voice of the next generation, remembers his first day as the voice of Orange Crush on the "Orange Crush Safety Club" program in 1949 when the usually mild-mannered Harry stormed out of the control room to set his pronunciation straight: "Never, EVER say the name of our sponsor that way!" he fumed. "It's not O-range Crush, it's just plain Ornjcrush. Got that? ORNJCRUSH — say that over several times and never forget it!!"[2]

The advertisers' exploitation of the airwaves in the Golden Age of Radio would last well into the 1950's when the growing popularity of television sealed its fate. Interestingly, and somewhat ironically, Harry Foster was quick to realize the potential of television; in fact, he was one of Canada's pioneers in promoting the very medium which would eventually doom radio's Golden Age. It was Grey Cup football which had much to do with Harry's shift in emphasis. Harry believed that what radio had done, television could do even better. The festivities of Grey Cup Week in November, which included the big parade which preceded the game itself, were in turn all preceded by a saturation of promotion and publicity which let Canadians know the preferred anti-freeze and the favourite electrical appliance.

The very first commercial TV program in Canada was another Foster first; it occurred in 1948, almost four years before the CBC got into television action. That first show consisted of two Foster-made films: "Royal Winter Fair" made for the Imperial Tobacco Company, and "Hockey Cavalcade" for the Walter M. Lowney Company. There were only a handful of television sets in Toronto and no broadcasting facility, so in a promotion for the newly opened "Times Square Lounge" in the King Edward Hotel,

[2] Martha Harron, *Don Harron. A Parent Contradiction* (Toronto: Collins, 1988), p.107.

The 1953 Grey Cup parade crosses Queen Street West going north on Bay Street in Toronto as part of Foster Advertising's promotion for the championship game.

Harry set up what was at the time an enormous nine-inch monitor for the show. He piped the programs around Lake Ontario from the transmitter at the newly opened WBEN-TV in Buffalo. This event gave the thousands of Torontonians who came to see this phenomenon their first real taste of television.

Between 1948 and 1952, American television grew at a spectacular pace while production in Canada lagged behind due to indecision and the lack of government funds. In Harry's mind, however, the medium was just around the corner and he was determined to be in on it the moment it was launched. To prepare for this moment, Harry vacated the King Edward Hotel in 1950 after planning new space in an office building constructed on Alcorn Avenue at Avenue Road, on property which he had owned for some time, just behind his old Oaklands home. While most agencies simply rented space in various office buildings, the new premises were built specifically for an advertising agency and contained spaces geared to the needs of each of the various advertising departments. Included, of course, were facilities to accommodate future television work. Another Foster first opened with two days of guided tours and festivities on the site.

In the meantime, Harry set about getting the football television rights in preparation for the day that television became a reality for Canadian football fans. That day arrived late in November, 1952, when for the first time in the history of Canadian football, the Grey Cup game between the Toronto Argonauts and the Edmonton Eskimos was televised over the CBC station in Toronto to an estimated 100,000 television sets. Since there was no link between Toronto and Montreal, the game was filmed and the film rushed by special plane to Montreal where it was broadcast on Montreal television the next day. Harry had made all the arrangements. Contracts were signed on behalf of Imperial Tobacco and Union Carbide who footed the bills, and dozens of personnel were organized to run the pre-game fanfare, the game itself and the post game wrap-ups. The commercials were created by Foster Advertising and put on 16mm film with Jack Dennett reading the words. Wes McKnight was the actual voice of the game, and the half-time show was dressed up with interviews which included Mayor Allen Lamport and local Member of Parliament, Lionel Conacher. There was also a special presentation to Ted Reeve of *The Telegram* for his long association with football. From Harry's point of view the whole production was designed as a spectacular state-of-the-art promotion. The program would get bigger and even more complicated in 1953 and 1954.

This first televised Grey Cup program did not go on the air without a hitch, however. The first commercial ever shown on purely Canadian television was run upside down and backwards by the CBC technicians! Harry, who was so meticulous when it came to organizational details, reeled in horror. Fortunately the CBC "made good" on the error and ran the entire game again along with Foster's commercials the next day. The whole exercise was a mammoth organisational task and an auspicious beginning for Canadian commercial television. It was also a far cry from 1931 when novice sportscaster Harry E. Foster had climbed to the roof of Varsity Stadium to give radio listeners over a twenty-odd

station network, a play-by-play description of a football game, reading the commercials himself and keeping his own statistics — all without a half-time break!

The high point of the Foster Agency in television was reached in 1954 when Harry completed exhausting negotiations between advertisers, sports authorities and the CBC for the telecast of the Commonwealth Games to be held in Vancouver in the summer as well as for the CFL games in the fall and the Grey Cup final. On behalf of the co-sponsors, the Northern Electric and the National Carbon companies, this was the biggest commercial program package ever undertaken for sports events in Canada up to that time. Harry did much of the leg work himself chalking up air miles and ironing out endless details. For the Commonwealth Games, a chain of newly built microwave relays from Vancouver to Los Angeles, to New York, to Buffalo, to Toronto and to Montreal had to be organized to bring the program eastwards since there were no transmission lines yet across the Rocky Mountains. For the first time, Canadians from coast to coast saw an event (including the famous Bannister-Landy sub four-minute mile) as it was actually happening. This was truly television history in the making and a red-letter day for the Foster Agency.

What Harry believed that he was proving in television was that private enterprise and advertising could get the job done by building on those win-win situations which were so much a part of his experience. The public would get good Canadian programs, the advertisers' sales curves would soar upward, and the Agency would reap its profits. That bright-looking future, however, would not materialize. The 1954 sports package was his last, as the CBC was actually gearing up for more of its own sports coverage. The next year they simply out-bid Harry's private network interests, effectively ending that chapter of his agency's business. Harry himself, the spokesman for free enterprise and promotional advertising, would long remember that watershed as one of the greatest disappointments in his public life.

In retrospect, the undermining of the television promotion side of the Agency might have been a blessing in

Harry's mother, Helen, and his brother, Jackie, stand in front of the family cottage at Wilcox Lake in the early 1940's.

disguise. The big dollars that would soon be needed for programming were beyond the resources of Harry's agency and most of his client advertisers. In any event, Harry Foster had a knack for weathering disappointments and rebounding to new endeavours. This setback was no exception. Radio and television advertisements would continue to be a staple of his agency's workload, but the programming days were definitely over. It would be to its strengths as a more traditional advertiser and promoter that Foster Advertising would turn its complete attention and reap its greatest rewards.

When the franchise was granted to Foster Advertising in 1944, Harry had fewer than thirty employees and only four major clients. Agency billings charged to clients (the yardstick in measuring agency size) were under $400,000 that first year. Twenty years later in 1964, with nearly three hundred employees, billings were beyond the $20 million mark, and Foster Advertising had established a reputation as being Canada's fastest growing agency. Within that first twenty years, Fosters had risen from the bottom to the number three position in the ranks of all agencies, and it had been necessary to add a third floor to the Alcorn Avenue office building.

While the first couple of years of formal agency operation were quite successful, two personal tragedies temporarily took some of the steam out of Harry's activities. First, Harry's mother died suddenly at home in July 1945. Helen Foster had always been the centre of the close-knit household and had been the person who had looked after the needs of brother Jackie since his birth in 1911. For Harry, the loss was immense. Soon after the funeral, he began his almost daily visits to the family home when he was in town, to walk around the block with Jackie, literally in his mother's footsteps. Harry's father looked after Jackie as best he could but eventually live-in nurses had to be hired.

Then in December 1946, Harry's wife Jimmie was riding her horse near the old Eglinton Hunt Club on the shoulder of an icy Don Mills Road when the animal balked at an oncoming truck. The startled horse reared onto the roadway and rolled over her, inflicting a fractured skull and numerous internal injuries. Jimmie's injuries took a long time to heal and, sadly, she was never the same again. Heroically, Harry devoted the rest of his life to caring for her. There would be no children to carry on the Foster name.

Harry did not talk freely to his colleagues about either of the misfortunes of 1945 and 1946, and there are no Foster diaries to tell us what deeper effect the tragedies had on the forty-year-old executive. These misfortunes, and Jackie's continued care, were certainly factors in Harry's eventual decision to launch projects to help the disabled. They also contributed to the transition Harry was already making in these years to a more conservative blue-suit approach to life, more appropriate to the business establishment of which he was now a part. His acceptance in 1945 into the prestigious Albany Club on King Street suggests too that the rambunctious stage of his life was behind him.

The Albany, founded by Sir John A. Macdonald himself, was the stronghold of the Conservative Party in the Toronto area. While Harry's political leanings had always been on the Conservative side, he certainly foresaw that appropriate contacts within the political establishment

Harry Foster and Prime Minister John Diefenbaker at the Albany Club in Toronto.

might be extremely helpful to his agency. The Club would also long continue to be a source of like-minded friendships and hearty luncheons close to his King Edward Hotel studios. With the earlier rambunctiousness quietly disappearing, it would be the ingrained promotional side of Harry's character which would come to the fore to create the success of his fledgling advertising business.

There were a number of reasons for the rapid growth of Foster Advertising in the two decades after 1945. One was the overall economic expansion of Canada itself in the post war world. Population and personal and national income were all leaping upward. New products, new ideas and new businesses were entering the market place by the thousands, and all were vying for visibility and a share of consumer preference. Any bright idea which would attract

Harry used models dressed in green and with dyed green hair in a campaign for Colgate's Chlorophyll Toothpaste in 1949-50.

attention was welcomed by clients.

Harry Foster had an uncanny sixth sense for smart ideas and an ability to spot trends before they materialized. It was because of this ability to come up with the big ideas, his infectious enthusiasm for marketing and promoting them and his many contacts in the business and sports worlds, that new business flowed into his agency. Harry also surrounded himself with talented people who could trans-

form big ideas into advertising reality. Harry himself was not afraid of hard work.

In the early years, many of his marketing ideas included door to door contact with consumers. He and his employees would canvass various neighbourhoods with products, small boxes of detergent for instance. A couple of weeks later, they would go back and try to sell another package. "That's how you find out about a product," he was quoted as saying. To launch Colgate's Chlorophyll Toothpaste, Harry dressed a number of models all in green, including green hair, and sent them around to pharmacies, radio stations and newspapers. The exposure and the unique approach made the promotion a success.

To secure the Smith Brothers Cough Drops account for Canada, Harry travelled to Quebec's eastern townships to research the Smith Brothers' Canadian ancestry and ended up participating in the company's centennial celebrations in the Poughkeepsie, New York head office. For that occasion, he presented himself in a *coureur de bois* outfit and a red beard matching the ones on the familiar label.

Maintaining accounts after they had been secured was also a major aspect of agency business. No advertising campaign lasts very long even today and the scramble for new ideas was then and still is an ongoing process. One of the fondest memories in the agency from the mid 1950's centred on a promotion for the Northern Electric Company,

Harry dressed up as a coureur de bois to celebrate the 100th anniversary of Smith Brothers, a cough drop manufacturer.

which was then entering the appliance business. They needed an idea to encourage sales among their dealers from coast to coast. Nothing was too good for Northern Electric in Harry's mind because this was his first big account as a new agency in 1944. They had not only handed him their business but also had provided him with his first branch office, right in their own Montreal headquarters.

Harry's solution in this case was to get Northern Electric to reward its highest-selling agents with football tickets in Vancouver. This necessitated renting a whole train and picking up the dealers and their wives on the way westward. When Harry discovered that there were no hotel spaces left due to the football game and that the passengers could not stay as intended on the railway siding for three days, the whole scheme was on the verge of collapse. The solution to the roadblock came at the last moment, when he bargained for a cruise ship to act as a hotel in the harbour. Also, to avoid offending either of the two national railways, and to maximize the favourable publicity for Northern Electric, the CPR train that carried the dealers out was replaced by a CN train to bring them back. Again, the result was a win-win situation.

On this occasion as on so many others, Harry's awareness of his clients' need to stay in the public eye paid interesting dividends. In 1969, when the whole country was in an uproar over the danger of cyclamates, the sugar substitute used in soft drinks, Harry's client, Canada Dry Limited, was stuck with warehouses full of soda pop that was unsaleable. The solution to Harry was simple: they would build an enormous pile of cans, rent a bulldozer and crush them all in public. In doing so, Canada Dry sacrificed a mountain of worthless pop for a mountain of excellent publicity!

In the days before video technology was available, the presentations of ideas to clients often resembled theatrical events. "Promoting an event requires the same basic approach as advertising; an original idea with a dash of showmanship," Harry always said. Today this is called the "dog and pony" approach. Back then, Harry referred to it as

Foster Advetising's successful promotion for their client, O'Keefe Brewers, juxtaposed a mounted knight with a modern sportscar at Casa Loma in Toronto.

"box office." Probably the most memorable of the early presentations revolved around the saving of the long-standing O'Keefe Brewing account. Threatening to fire the agency because of dipping market share, the company invited Foster's and one other agency to fight it out with presentations based on their established helmet and shield logo. Foster's came up with the idea of presenting a real man in armour (representing the time-honoured skills of the brew master) placed against a backdrop of contemporary scenes. The plan, requiring completion within three short weeks, gave rise to many humerous complications bringing Red Foster to his energetic best.

The first of these problems was in obtaining a real suit of armour. This was a difficult proposition in itself but Harry managed the impossible in a deal with the Royal Ontario Museum. They then had to find a horse and rider strong enough to carry the heavy armour. Because the colour of the horse also had to be just right, this led to a frantic search which, oddly enough, ended up in Harry's own stable. Next the armour proved to be too small for an ordinary non-medieval sized person, so a jockey had to be found. The jockey, however, couldn't climb onto the horse because of the weight of his suit, so a special stand had to be built.

A number of scenes were attempted to get just the right advertising flavour. One showed the horse and rider watching modern scuba divers emerging from Lake Ontario, but that almost came to grief when the horse refused to go near the water. Another scene was taken at the airport beside a modern CF100 aircraft. Arrangements with military officials were difficult and the noise was almost too much for the horse, which refused to stand still. A third attempt, showed the team with a modern gull-wing Mercedes in the courtyard of Casa Loma. An entourage of nearly twenty people — horse handlers, knight dressers, photographers, consultants, prop men, and so on, was needed to bring the knight "to life." These elaborate efforts involved considerable expense and long rehearsals for a handful of finished photographs, but the end result saved the account. And everyone in the agency had fun!

Other stories of Harry's sometimes "off the wall" approaches filtered through the various advertising agencies and usually confirmed his reputation as the *enfant terrible* of the Canadian advertising industry as well as one of Canada's best salesmen. Harry was sometimes referred to as a man who could sell a dead horse to a Mountie. He once erected a billboard near a prospective client's head office which said "We Want Your Business." Another time, he

The Royal Winter Fair was one of Foster's accounts during the 1940's, and the company's promotional work included setting up a stage on the grounds. The billboard on the right advertises a film of the Royal Tour of 1939 in which Harry had also been involved.

jumped out of a birthday cake during a presentation.

On yet another occasion, Harry went deliberately late to a meeting of a client and a number of potential ad agencies. He barged into the room, threw his hat on the table and announced, "Mine's in there too now!" One of the best illustrations of his persuasive powers occurred when he and his executives were driving to Kitchener to bid for the J. M. Schneider account. Just as they entered the city, the car broke down. Undaunted, Harry jumped out, flagged down the first car going in their direction and talked the bewildered motorist into taking the team and all its baggage right to the Schneider front door!

One important account which he won in 1952 and held for more than two decades was the Canadian National Exhibition. Harry probably enjoyed this one the most of any because of his early broadcasting connections with the "Ex" and the many opportunities it presented to provide the entertainment for millions of people. Harry Foster's Outdoor Theatre on the grounds had been the first of its kind in the late 1940's. From its stage, Harry had introduced the big stars of the day, broadcast the news, staged movies and shows, merchandised products, and generally kept the crowds entertained from morning to night. Along with the CNE's director of public relations, Harry Foster as advertising agent, can take much of the credit for the record breaking crowds which flocked to this gigantic fall fair in the 1950's and 1960's. The account itself fit perfectly with his philosophy that advertising services played an important role in the economic growth of the nation and Harry exploited the Exhibition for what it really was — a two week promotional bonanza.

On one occasion Harry obtained an enormous piece of stone from the Rock of Gibraltar on behalf of Prudential Insurance which in itself became a major attraction. In another promotion, this time for Colgate, Harry demonstrated his skill in tying in a number of his clients' products to create a bigger effect. He brought the famous dog, "Lassie" to appear in the grandstand show. This was accompanied by a "name the Lassie pup" contest using labels from Ajax cleanser and Palmolive soap, and by Northern Electric's washing machines and Trans Canada Airlines tickets for the winners. The exposure for the products was enormous. The whole promotion came very close to sliding off the rails, however, when Harry discovered, by accident, that Lassie was really a "he"! Harry never let on.

The association with the Exhibition also got Harry involved in the Canadian Sports Hall of Fame, which really started as an Exhibition promotion in 1955. His passion for sports, for Canadian achievement of all sorts, and for the spotlight, as well as his unique talent as a master of ceremonies led eventually to his becoming the Chairman of that institution in 1975. In this capacity he made a valuable contribution too. One of his first goals was to acquire the services of a full-time curator to look after the collection. Then, over the years, Harry pushed for numerous and essential physical renovations that made the building one of the most interesting in North America at the time for the display of Canada's sporting memorabilia. The Sports Hall of Fame continues to this day to induct Canada's sporting heroes and to present The Lou Marsh Memorial Trophy to Canada's athlete of the year.

Even though his own advertising methods were working admirably in the 1950's and the Agency's growth curve continued its upward momentum, Harry was always conscious of the need to stay current with the way advertisers did business. In many respects, Harry believed that he was leading the way, and his speeches at the time confirm this.

By 1958, he had a unique four-man market research department in place at the agency, and in 1959 he inaugurated a series of marketing seminars at the University of Toronto. In these, executives from Foster client companies worked through case studies with experts and with the help of a computer which, at that time, was certainly a novel approach. Harry was also aware that some of Canada's best business brains often fled to the United States in search of better opportunities, a fact that grated on his sense of Canadianism. To help combat this problem (and to add to

Foster visibility) he sponsored a number of post-graduate scholarships in marketing studies at Western, Queens and Toronto. In his view, advertising had unlimited potential on home ground.

The expansion of the Foster Agency in the 1960's was helped measurably by the acquisition of a large slice of the prestigious General Motors account in 1962. It was not a "dog and pony" show that had won that business; GM had simply chosen Foster after a two-year investigation of various agencies. Their decision was based on the qualities of the organization that Harry had built into it by that time — stability in Canada, depth and strength of people in the agency itself, research ability, a cross-Canada network of branch offices, and the high profile charitable work which even by 1962 was a Foster hallmark. Harry was tremendously proud of the GM achievement. Aside from its value as an agency showcase and the excitement and financial reward it generated, it seemed to justify the hard work of many years.

Equally satisfying was his 1966 award as Ad Man of the Year and the Gold Medal from the Association of Canadian Advertisers. This prestigious award was given in recognition of the highest standards of achievement by any agency and of the major role Harry had played in opening up what had always been a rather stuffy elite group to include everyone in the advertising business. This aspect was a clear reflection of Harry's vision of advertising playing a key role in the continuing economic growth of the whole country. When he actually received the award, he did so on crutches and against his doctor's advice. More than three months before on an Arizona holiday, Harry was helping to unsaddle his horse when the horse kicked him just above the knee splintering his thigh. There was fear that he would never walk properly again. This accident led to three months of traction and agonizing physiotherapy. Receiving that Gold Medal was both a triumph of personal physical determination as well as a triumph of his agency's achievement.

Canada's Centennial Year, 1967, was filled with projects

Harry receives the 1966 award for Advertising Man of the Year presented by the Association of Canadian Advertisers. Harry accepted the award even through he was recuperating from an accident in which he was kicked by a horse.

of all sizes to mark the occasion. The Foster Agency was responsible for promoting the famous "Discovery Train" which criss-crossed the nation carrying the story of Canada's history. The year was also marked with the opening of a new Foster Building on St. Clair Avenue in mid-town Toronto after two years of planning. The agency had long outgrown the old Alcorn offices and the new gleaming white structure was Harry's method of maintaining a high degree of public visibility for the agency.

Foster Advertising's office building at St. Clair Avenue west of Yonge Street in Toronto was crowned with a rotating logo.

The fourteen floors were topped with an enormous revolving gyroscope; this was Harry's idea of providing a symbol to highlight the balanced nature of his business. The grand opening took three full days of gala events and visitations which, in retrospect, would mark the last of Harry Foster's showbiz agency presentations. The fact that the gyroscope suffered numerous mechanical breakdowns became a source of minor frustration over the next several years, but the building itself, still close to his Cottingham Square roots, was a proud mark of personal achievement.

By 1969, the agency's 25th anniversary, Foster Adver-tising was serving more companies than any other agency in Canada. His clients included General Motors, B. F. Goodrich, Ontario Hydro, Air Canada, Canada Dry, Colgate-Palmolive, O'Keefe Brewing Company, The Royal Bank and over two hundred others of smaller stature. Everyone in the agency took real pride in the fact that more than one-quarter of the accounts had been with Fosters for over fifteen years and two accounts, Northern Electric and Lowneys, had been associated for twenty-five years. Loy-alty of clients and loyalty among agency personnel were important ingredients in Harry's notion of success. His was the third largest agency in the industry and was fast closing on the number two spot.

At this time, however, Harry was 64 years old and rumours were flying that he was about to retire altogether and devote full time to the many interests which he had accumulated over the years. These included the Associa-tion for Retarded Children, the Grey Cup Dinner Commit-tee, the Canadian National Institute for the Blind, St. Michael's Hospital, the Boy Scouts Association, St. Jude's Anglican Church in Oakville, the Canadian Paraplegic Association, the Charlie Conacher Dinners for Cancer Research, and The Lou Marsh Selection Committee for the Outstanding Canadian Athlete of the year at Canada's Sports Hall of Fame. Harry was President of the Albany Club from 1965 through 1968, perhaps the busiest years of his life, yet he also found time to serve on the boards of several companies and on the board at his old school, Ridley College. The changes in the whole nature of the advertising business, however, were slowly turning Harry Foster, the active and fun-loving player, into Harry Foster the manager which, however necessary, was not a role that really suited his temperament.

One interesting example of the way that the approach to advertising was changing in the early 1970's occurred in the summer of 1972 when the excitement over the Canada-Russia hockey series was beginning to build. At stake were enormous sums of money to be paid by advertisers for their few minutes of on-air television exposure. Early in June, it

Harry Foster presents the Lou Marsh Trophy for Canada's Athlete of the Year to Elaine Tanner in 1966.

was assumed that MacLarens would handle the whole series for $500,000. Then in a not-so-strange alliance between Harold Ballard of Maple Leaf Gardens fame who was as anxious as anyone to see a Russian defeat and Alan Eagleson, the founder of the NHL Players Association, the two combined forces and offered $750,000 for the rights to sell all the advertising. Ballard had Maple Leaf Gardens stock as collateral and Eagleson was using Bobby Orr's money although Orr was unaware of the fact. They then asked Harry Foster to line up the sponsors based on the $750,000 bid.

With the support of his major clients, Canadian Breweries Limited, Canada Dry and the Royal Bank, Harry set out to fill the advertising time. He believed that Foster Advertising had priority rights since they were the first agency to support the Ballard/Eagleson bid with a firm offer. By July, with the increasing interest in the hockey series which translated into more viewers and thus higher advertising rates, a war of sorts broke out among various

corporate advertisers who began to bid up the prices.

Harry, speaking on behalf of his clients, was upset by what he considered to be the unbusinesslike dealings of playing client against client after a deal, although not yet signed, had been made. Always conscious of the fact that he was in a business which spent other people's money, and coming from an era when a handshake was as good as a signed document, Harry was bothered by this bidding war. He was not prepared for this new form of wheeling and dealing and he and his clients were soon forced out of the fight.

This incident, while disappointing, was not an agency

After years of work, Harry Foster's advertising agency becomes one of the largest and most successful in Canada.

Harry Foster stands with the group of long term employees who would take over control of the company in 1973. They are Denis Jotcham, Douglas Turnbull, Arthur Collins, Harry Foster, Alan Purves, and Fred DeGuerre.

crisis. It occurred at least two years after Harry had already decided what he was going to do with the enterprise he had built, and what he ended up doing was unique in the annals of Canadian business. Resisting the possibilities of mergers with other agencies and the ever present threat of takeovers from American advertising agencies, he gradually set plans in motion to transfer the ownership of the entire operation to a group of capable, senior long-term employees.

This process took nearly three years to complete but when the formal transfer ceremonies occurred in February of 1973, Harry Foster could be assured that Foster Advertising remained a 100% Canadian owned firm. Harry stayed on as Honorary Chairman of the Board until 1976 and helped with accounts where he could but he was content to hope that his successors could fulfil the dream of becoming the number one agency in Canada. Heading the new Foster Agency was Arthur Collins, a ten year veteran of the agency. "Nice guys do win, you see," Harry commented at the time, " [Collins] is an excellent administrator with a great ability to listen to people. Underneath, however, there

is a hard core of toughness." Harry might have been delivering a small part of his own eulogy!

It seemed as if Harry Foster had done it all even by 1969. He had built a multi-million dollar enterprise and had come close to the very top of the industry he loved so much. A lifetime on the promotional front would surely be enough for any one man. Harry had earned the right to retire to his wilderness retreat in Quebec to pursue his love for fishing, flowers and photography. Not surprisingly, however, there would be other and perhaps even more dramatic chapters in his career. He would devote his remarkable energies toward another organization in his life, the Foster Foundation, a trust set up in the early years of the agency to finance charitable work. The flamboyant techniques of the advertising business would come to the fore again, and the Foundation would achieve wonders for the cause of mentally disabled children in Canada. This interest, which had its roots in the experiences of his brother and the love of his mother, would add the words "humanitarian" and "philanthropist" to Harry's already full biography.

Chapter Eight
Crusade

From his earliest childhood, Harry Foster had gained his understanding of the problems associated with mental disabilities from first hand experience with his younger brother Jackie. The six years in age that separated the two brothers made no apparent difference to the relationship. Jackie was a special case for sure, but he was always an integral part of the close knit Foster family. Harry had been raised in a family which understood completely the capacity of disabled people to love and to be loved, and which rejected totally any notion of hiding the boy in an institution. The high board fence that surrounded the back yard was the only protection from the outside world the family permitted.

Moreover, the example set by Harry's mother in caring for Jackie in her daily walks around the neighbourhood in the face of public misunderstanding and in the firmness of her resolve to keep the family together at all costs had a permanent influence on young Harry. There is no doubt that without these influences, the life and career of Harry Foster would have been quite different. As it turned out, the family's unique situation at 4 Oaklands Avenue, coupled with Harry's genius for business and promotion, was another fortunate combination, one which yielded enormous dividends for mentally handicapped people everywhere.

More direct involvement in the affairs of disabled people in general and of mentally disabled people in particular came for Harry in the years just after World War Two. Both his mother's death in 1945 and his wife's riding accident in 1946 forced a reorganization of priorities in Harry's life. He made a deathbed promise to his mother to look after Jackie, a promise which he would honour many times over. Jackie Foster, however, was destined to remain on the sidelines for most of his life, and he would not be the beneficiary of the advances made for mentally disabled people in the post-war decades. Jimmie Foster's accident necessitated months of rehabilitation and months of anxiety for Harry about her long term chances of recovery. She too would remain partly on the sidelines, loved and cared for, but less prominent in the mainstream of Harry's public life. Coupling these difficulties with the demands and challenges of the newly enfranchised advertising agency, there would be few spare moments in Harry's daily schedule in those early post-war years to think much beyond his immediate concerns let alone to act on behalf of all handicapped people.

For physically disabled people in general and the mentally handicapped in particular, the 19th century and much of the 20th were wasted years. There were no nurseries, schools, residences or training facilities. Periodically, a few strong voices were raised against the legacy of inhumanity toward those who were referred to as the "feeble minded." The general public's ignorance and misunderstanding lumped people with mental disabilities and the mentally ill together. Occasionally, the concerns of the disabled regarding the absence of facilities, programs and the general lack of governmental will to deal with the issue were raised. For the most part, those voices of concern fell on deaf ears due to strong prevailing negative social attitudes and the absence of consistent government direction or policy. The Great Depression, followed by increased pressures on society during World War Two, doomed any efforts on behalf of Canada's disabled.

Daniel, Jackie, and Harry stand outside Harry's home in Oakville in 1951 or 1952.

As tragic as the war was in so many ways, one positive consequence became apparent even before the conflict ended when the hundreds of newly disabled warriors began returning to Canada. Attention was quickly drawn to the need for action on behalf of men who had made enormous sacrifices in the cause of freedom. Fortunately, the government's response to those veterans was both direct and purposeful, reflecting a society which, on the whole, had become far more responsive to human distress than it had been after World War One.

Leading the way in pressing the Department of Veterans Affairs for affirmative action was the Canadian Paraplegic Association which was incorporated early in 1945. Behind that organization was a group of dedicated physicians and veterans themselves and among the latter group was John G. Counsell, a spinal cord casualty from the Dieppe Raid in 1942. Counsell was a courageous individual who refused to give in to his own despair and became determined that people like himself, forever in wheelchairs, could not only learn how to prolong their lives but also how to live independently and productively. In this endeavour, his pioneering efforts met with remarkable long-term success.

Encouraging him along the way was his friend Harry Foster. Harry and John were both men of action, both shared the bonds of Ridley College days and successful pre-war football and business careers, and both were of a temperament to support each other's causes although neither interfered with the other. What Harry undoubtedly learned from their post-war association was the notion that disabled people could indeed be helped to help themselves. This was a seed sown in Harry's mind which complemented the influences already at work in his own life. Progress made in one area would inevitably promote progress in another.

In the field of mental disabilities, it was not until the late 1940's that any real advances were made and, as in the work with paraplegics and amputees, the early steps were often hesitant. These would gain momentum rapidly in the 1950's, however, as new ideas about treatment caught fire. Progress in the care for mentally disabled people had its beginnings, not with flashing lights and thundering speeches from government officials, but in a grass-roots movement sparked by the parents themselves. Their main concern was the need for education for their children who by law were excluded from neighbourhood schools.

In Kirkland Lake, Ontario, in 1947, the first tiny school for disabled children appeared. Within a year, a Toronto group of like-minded parents had formed itself into an association, holding meetings, sharing information and talking about how to get the kind of services, particularly in education, that they felt were needed. Within five years, there were eighteen such local associations across Ontario, and these were linked in a province-wide network called the Ontario Association for Retarded Children (OARC), which was incorporated in 1953. By 1956, forty-three associations had mushroomed in Ontario alone and an umbrella body, the Canadian Association for Retarded Children (CARC) was firmly in place to co-ordinate efforts on a national scale. Early association meetings took place in people's homes or in church basements, and basic funds for such organizational necessities as stamps, newsletter duplication, and office space were always major hurdles. To operate a basement school required herculean effort by volunteers. Trained teachers were in short supply and the leadership, however dedicated, often lacked the expertise necessary to conduct affairs on a professional level, something which would be necessary if the general public and especially the government were ever to be jolted into supporting the movement.

Harry Foster and his father attended some of the early meetings of the Toronto Association, but Harry was reported to have been a rather quiet member. While he had little to say at first, his understanding of the many broader problems which the Association was identifying was certainly deepening, and he did get to know a growing number of the people involved. The statistics on the growth of the local associations that were springing up across Canada always amazed him. Like-minded people were finally coming forward to band together to effect progress. By the early 1950's, Harry's involvement had become more active. His talents as a public speaker at the gatherings of local associations were the first to be noticed, and it was not long before his organizational abilities emerged as well. He had seen that the movement's potential extended far beyond his family's concerns at 4 Oaklands Avenue.

As a volunteer and one already prominent in business and entertainment circles, Harry's speeches on the subject of mental disabilities were far from thundering or militant. Instead, they were carefully researched, sincere masterpieces which relied on a high degree of earnest persuasion and honest passion. His themes were completely in accord with the stated goals of the movement which was dedicated to promoting assistance to mentally disabled children everywhere in hopes of their becoming more self-sufficient and self-supporting. As John Counsell was discovering with the Canadian Paraplegic Association in the early 1950's, Harry and the various associations were coming to realize that the achievement of these goals would involve enormous effort across a broad spectrum of issues. These included education, training, development of personnel, research and funding. Harry was about to make a gigantic contribution in many of these areas, particularly in the one which worked at breaking down the wall of public ignorance which was at the heart of the problem. Here was a cause which was tailor-made for the business expertise he could bring to bear, for the financial support which he was becoming more and more capable of offering, and for his connections with people in high places that were part and parcel of the advertising world.

While ignorance and misunderstanding about mental disabilities were (and are) long term problems, the actual financing of the movement's immediate organizational needs was the most critical in the early 1950's. Most parents were simply not able to do things such as research and long-range planning, things that would be required of a national organization.

It was here, especially, that Harry Foster had something to offer. To assist these longer range goals, Harry established the Harry E. Foster Foundation in 1954. This was an unusual business decision which reflected his growing success in the advertising world as well as his growing zeal to make a long term financial contribution to the cause. The Foundation was a means of channelling a high percentage of the profits from the Foster Advertising Agency into a trust fund, whose proceeds could be used to finance many projects.

It was another win-win-win situation. Harry could legally avoid some of the heavy taxation on his business, and at the same time give personal direction to the way the money was spent. The emphasis of the Foundation was in initiating and stimulating pilot projects. Harry termed this sort of giving as "seed money," a term which reflected everyone's hopes, and the "sower of seeds" became the theme of his Foundation's logo. Early grants were small and were initially spread among a number of worthy causes, including the Canadian Paraplegic Association, but as the years passed they centered more and more on projects for mentally disabled people.

The latter half of the 1950's was truly a building period

The logo for the Harry E. Foster Charitable Foundation symbolized Harry's vision of charity as the sower of seeds.

in Canada for the Foster Foundation, for Harry's advertising agency, and for the increasing numbers of local, provincial and national associations that worked on behalf of the disabled. With the growth of the movement came the inevitable mushrooming of projects based on real needs at all levels. The Foundation came to the rescue many times in a variety of ways during these years, including providing the first year's salary for OARC's provincial Executive Director, the underwriting of long-range surveys and planning conferences, the establishment of the first office for the National Association in one of Harry's residential properties in Toronto, and the organization of the first of many province-wide fund-raising campaigns. Harry himself organized and directed these very successful drives for

money and public awareness, and they all benefited from the flair that was typical of the Foster Advertising Agency's methodical techniques of planning, research and presentation.

In 1956, Harry put himself even more into the spotlight with the production of a short film entitled *The Lady on My Street.* He persuaded his friend Lorne Greene from the radio world to introduce the subject and, into the film's short ten minutes, Harry managed to package a moving and powerful appeal which brought together the social problem of mental disabilities, the philosophy of the Association at the time, and the urgent need for action.

Harry had chosen to feature himself in the film, partly because of his own strong desire to move public opinion forward by bringing a higher degree of visibility to the whole problem and partly because there was simply no other prominent public figure in Canadian society at the time who could deliver such a message. The film itself was shown countless times across the country and abroad, and it proved to be a powerful force in changing public attitudes. The script, too, was often printed in newspapers and in Association literature. What was not readily apparent, to viewers or readers who did not know Harry, was that the story was really about his own family. The "Lady" was Harry's mother. The film ended on a personal and biblical note:

So that is why it is a privilege to belong to an organization that helps tie shoelaces, an organization that will go into the houses, into the upper rooms and help them down the stairs, bring them from behind the high board fences, take them by the hands, and lead them out into the sunshine and make real for them, and those yet unborn, the words of Him who said: "Inasmuch as ye have done it unto the least of these, my brethren, ye have done it unto me."

Harry's growing commitment to the movement, the early work of the Foster Foundation, and the production of

The Lady on My Street, coincided with a strong religious period in his life. There had always been a religious orientation in the Foster family, but not in a particularly church-going way. Jimmie Foster was a Roman Catholic, and Harry himself attended a variety of churches when they lived in Toronto. After they moved to Oakville in 1950, Harry settled at St. Jude's Anglican Church, where he and the rector developed a long friendship. Harry cultivated a broad interest in many subjects including religion, and he would often jot down ideas or expressions on his ever-present note pad, at church or anywhere else, for recall and discussion at a later time.

His interest in religion led to his confirmation in 1957 in the Anglican Church at the age of 52. Desiring this aspect of his life to be as private as possible, he chose to stand with the boys being confirmed at his old alma mater, Ridley College in St. Catharines, something he had not been prepared to do back in 1924. The strength of his religious beliefs was undoubtedly a great help when, late in 1957, his father, "D. H." died suddenly at the age of 80, right in the office that he had occupied at the Agency for so long. The memorial gifts went directly to the Ontario Association which eased the grief somewhat but Harry had lost not only a business confidant but also a great and close friend. His brother Jackie would now be at home alone with private nursing care, alone except for Red's daily visits when he was in town.

At the time of his father's death, Harry was in the middle of a campaign to recruit leadership talent for public service work from within the ranks of all of the advertising agencies. He believed that agency people had special skills in speaking, budgeting and motivating the public, which could somehow be pooled for everyone's benefit. When he went as far as suggesting that all the advertising agencies adopt mental disabilities as their collective cause, (much like the fire fighters whose main charitable concern is Muscular Dystrophy), the whole idea collapsed before it got off the ground. In the competitive world of advertising, firms were not ready for this sort of co-operation and most

Harry Foster organised the Christmas party at the Wellesley Street School. As was typical of his style, he asked local celebrities like Walter "Turk" Broda of the Toronto Maple Leafs to attend.

already had their own designated projects.

It could not be said, however, that Harry Foster was being naive when he sought this sort of co-operation in his own industry. He honestly believed that mental disabilities were not only a legitimate and important cause, but also one which every right-thinking person should adopt because the need was so obvious. As well, this cause had a profile high enough for the visibility that advertising agencies all relished. There is also a likelihood that Harry saw a possibility of heading this scheme himself. The failure of his initiative within the ad industry, however, was not taken as a terrible blow. To him, it was simply a bright idea whose day had not yet dawned.

Harry Foster was a product of a generation where

executives donated to charity as a matter of course, partly because they could afford to do so and partly because the government was not yet very active in social causes and did not smother businesses with high taxation. Conn Smythe of the Toronto Maple Leafs with disabled children, for instance, was typical of those executives. His generation believed that private enterprise could get the job done, although after the mid 1950's, it was becoming clear to most that this was an impossible daydream. Harry's own record of personal contributions to charities other than those focusing on mental disabilities is astonishing in its length and for the anonymous way in which much of it was done.

The Christmas Party for disabled children, for instance, at the Wellesley Street School, which he organized for many years, went purposely unheralded. This was simply the way these things got done. Sharing some laughs and generally having fun with kids, of course, was an old and genuine Foster gift . Sharing that gift was something that Harry truly enjoyed. With these things in mind, it is not surprising that Foster Advertising would be an industry leader in corporate support for charity. When government purse strings did begin to open a bit in the 1960's, in response to a recognition of real needs and thanks to enormous pressures from a great many organizations, Harry would be at the front of the line, adding his own voice to the pressure on high places as well as seeking assistance for his cause.

The idea of industry co-operation, corporate charity and of pressing the governments of the day for help was entirely in keeping with a Foster principle, mounted on a plaque in Harry's office as a daily reminder. It stated: "You can accomplish anything as long as you don't care who gets the credit." Harry believed this wholeheartedly even though he would be criticized at times for stealing the limelight and for his chronic compulsion to be in charge of things. The criticism did bother him although he was never a person to show negative emotions. He masked these anxieties, however, always firm in his belief that what he was doing was for the cause and certainly not for himself.

This belief was reflected in Harry's constant use of the pronoun "we" when referring to himself in conversations, and was also part of the reason Harry Foster was famous for his thank-you notes and flowers. Preparations for Christmas always began in October and his card and gift list ran to a dozen closely typed pages. All of the notes and cards which have survived show clearly that the recipients were always made to feel that they were an important part of something much bigger. One sample from 1938 shows that Red's "thank-you" style emerged early in his career. Complementing a *Globe and Mail* executive for participating in his popular Mutt Contest, he wrote:

What you did the other night reminded me so much of the cooperation of Lou Marsh, that I just wanted you to know aside from any newspaper tie-ups that your assistance was sincerely appreciated. You know, writing about something is one thing and really being interested is another, and the way you came down from the table and helped to give out buttons was "something."

This practice of sending notes, which only got better and more prolific over the years, demonstrates a strong streak of sentimentality in Harry's character which often shone brighter than the sportsman/executive image he had cultivated. Cynics, of course, could argue that this behaviour was all promotion and set-up for the next tap on the shoulder, but the sheer quantity and the sincerity of Harry's messages belie this. There was a graciousness about the way Harry conducted himself which led many people not to mind being buttered up, especially for a good cause. In the area of fund raising, this talent was crucial.

The first large-scale effort to raise money in a highly visible way came in 1960. Harry believed by then that the general public was ready for a campaign on a grand scale, and that a telethon blitz would serve the purpose. The opportunity presented itself when fellow business entre-

FIRST NATIONAL MEETING, CARC BOARD OF HONORARY GOVERNORS, 2nd OCTOBER, 1964

The first national meeting of the Canadian Centennial Crusade for the Mentally Retarded representatives held on October 2, 1964 at the Granite Club in Toronto. As Chairman of the Board of Honorary Governors, Harry Foster (centre front) was able to marshal support for the project from his many business associates.

preneur and owner of *The Toronto Telegram*, John Bassett Sr., was preparing to launch his new television station, CFTO-TV, in January of 1961. Harry convinced his friend that the best way to inaugurate the station would be a giant program (and corporate donation of time) on behalf of mentally handicapped people. After a mere three weeks of planning and organization by the two executives, what hit the airwaves on New Year's Day was an eighteen-hour television spectacular described in the press as a gold-plated, good natured marathon. As one witness expressed it, the telethon was "like trying to launch D-Day while an Olympiad was being held in the same place."[3]

Harry had coaxed dozens of volunteers and celebrities to be part of the show. In all, over five hundred personalities crossed the stage during the program. There were singers, dancers, cowboys, air cadets, archers, newsmen, children, a helicopter and fireworks. Station president Joel Aldred kept the proceedings flowing and all of the special guests, including the *Telegram* Sports Editor Jim Vipond and the

Globe columnist Bruce West, two of Harry's best friends, spoke on the theme of giving. Harry, of course, added his own sincere appeal and then put $1,000 into the pot himself.

This was all pure promotion, and for the older members of the viewing audience, it was clearly reminiscent of the glitz of the Victory Bond rallies Harry had engineered during World War Two. The only thing that was really new was the use of electronics. The exposure that the concerns of people with mental disabilities received that day was of inestimable value. The first donation on the program was in fact Harry's own $25,000, although it was made anonymously as far as the public was concerned. The OARC realized over $210,000 for their programs in a single day.

There is no doubt that the success of the telethon did much to confirm Harry's belief that even bigger plans for the movement were in order. The 1950's had brought noticeable progress in both public and professional understanding of the issue of mental disabilities. That much more could be done for the majority of the more than 600,000

---

[3] Alex Barris, *The Pierce-Arrow Showroom is Leaking* (Toronto: Ryerson, 1969), p.63.

As Harry Foster looks on, Prime Minister Lester B. Pearson presents a scrapbook of newspaper stories covering the success of the Canadian John F. Kennedy Memorial Fund to Sargent Shriver, Executive Director of the Kennedy Foundation.

mentally disabled persons in Canada was becoming clearer with each medical breakthrough and advance in treatment. The hope generated by the announcement of the vaccine against polio in 1954, for instance, was one of a number of breakthroughs in the decade which encouraged optimism in many medical fields. That optimism carried over into the 1960's and was clearly reflected in Harry's speeches.

In 1963, Harry took it upon himself to see what the rest of the world was doing on the mentally disabled front. He, along with small delegations, visited England, Ireland and the United States where unique projects were already in operation. Based on armloads of reports from these projects,

he then decided to organize an Honorary Board of Governors for the Canadian Association and, in his capacity as Chairman, he set out again, with the aid of the Royal Bank's executive jet, this time across each province, to solicit more ideas and support for the grand attack on the whole range of problems involving mental disabilities which was slowly formulating in his mind. As Chairman of the Honorary Board, and using his vast network of contacts, he got himself into the offices of the chairmen and presidents of corporations, of the leaders in the mental disabilities field, of educational circles and of research establishments, literally selling the idea for a grand attack to each one personally. He eventually secured the participation of nearly two hundred leaders in key areas.

What this group decided to launch in the summer of 1964 was a crusade on a scale never before envisioned or attempted. The ideas, which formed first in Harry's mind and then crystallized with the input of many other minds, came to be known as the Centennial Crusade for the Mentally Retarded. It was purposely designed to coincide with the hundreds of other Canadian Centennial projects which were set in motion that year to celebrate the 100th birthday of the nation.

What emerged from the planning of the Honorary Board was a series of ten (and eventually fourteen) major research and training projects. Speaking as the Chairman of the Honorary Board of Governors to launch the plan, Harry was quoted as believing that the Crusade would be "a more fitting monument in 1967 than any centennial gift to Canada wrought in stone or steel; it is concerned with life, and a better living for that three percent of the Canadian population who are mentally retarded."

What was launched was also the product of certain other events which had come together at this particular time in Harry's life to fashion another of those fortunate combinations of his. These events occurred in the months prior to the launching of the Centennial Crusade and they added a sense of urgency to the whole project. One of the secrets of Harry Foster's promotional success was his unique ability to turn a news event of any sort into an idea either to sell a product, to raise money or to involve and encourage volunteers. This was a talent cultivated in the early advertising days, and it continued to be very useful in the cause of mental disability.

Late in November, 1963, when the world was shaken by the assassination of U.S. President John Kennedy, Harry moved quickly to establish The Canadian John F. Kennedy Memorial Fund. It seemed at the time simply to be the right thing to do. This fund recognized the valuable leadership given by the late President in making the battle against mental disabilities a focus of his administration. Harry organized the publicity and the public was invited to contribute through the chartered banks. The first $10,000 donation was a Foster Foundation gift, and eventually, more than $100,000 in donations were raised for research and program development in Canada. The world had lost a dynamic leader, but the cause of mentally disabled people had made another tremendous gain through Harry's quick reaction to a tragedy. Valuable links had also been forged with the Kennedy Foundation.

Early in 1964, yet another tragedy was turned to the benefit of the movement when Jackie Foster fell out of bed, breaking bones in his ankles. This was a shock which his fragile body could not take and after a few restless days in the hospital, he died at the age of 52. Jackie Foster would live on through Harry's efforts on his behalf. Already underway at the time of Jackie's death was a project to create a library and research centre at the CARC's National Headquarters in Toronto. Memorial funds for Jackie from Harry's friends and from the Foundation were immediately directed to completing that project and late in January 1964, the plaque was unveiled inaugurating the John Orr Foster Memorial Library for Mental Retardation.

Out of the tragedies came opportunities which made 1964 and 1965 whirlwind years for Harry. Plans for the new Foster Building on St. Clair Avenue were underway, and the Centennial Crusade absorbed enormous amounts of organizational, travel and public speaking time, but Harry was in his element. The financing of the various provincial

The plaque which marks the inauguration of a national research library at the headquarters of the Canadian Association for Retarded Children is dedicated to Harry's brother Jackie. This library is now part of the Roeher Institute at York University.

centennial projects for the disabled had to get started so that they would be functioning in 1967, and Harry maintained a keen interest in all of these. He even worked directly in Manitoba, for instance, in getting all of the General Motors dealers to lend their support to that province's Crusade project, a research facility for handicapped people in Brandon. There were also numerous trips to Ottawa to get the government bodies on side, and dozens of luncheons with corporate leaders in the Foster network. The most painstaking effort, however, went into the planning for the

The official launch of the Canadian Centennial Crusade at the Royal York Hotel in Toronto brought together such luminaries as (from left to right) Lorne Greene, Rose Kennedy, John Robarts and Harry Foster (kneeling).

official launching of the Crusade set for September 1965, at the Royal York Hotel in Toronto. What Harry organized for that occasion was a promotional masterpiece which went far beyond the normal Foster standards for such things.

If the fight to benefit mentally disabled people was to be significantly advanced, it seemed logical to Harry to get the biggest names possible associated with it. Ever mindful of the tie-in potential, Harry set the dinner date to coincide with the visit of Governor General Georges Vanier to

Toronto to open the new City Hall. He knew that the ribbon-cutting would be an afternoon affair leaving the evening open for the Vaniers.

When the participation of the Governor General was confirmed, Harry then decided to turn the launching of the $15,000,000 Crusade into a dinner for Mrs. Rose Kennedy, mother of the late President and also the mother of a mentally disabled daughter, to honour her for her work with the American cause. The attendance of these two big names would be the lever in securing Prime Minister Lester Pearson, and the Premier of Ontario, John Robarts, as well. These leaders would all make very public affirmations of the desire of their governments to become involved in the movement.

When the arrangements were completed, the Head Table alone would feature fifty of the country's most prominent figures and their spouses. Political figures, church leaders, chairmen of the Provincial Crusades, corporate leaders and Harry's old friend now of Hollywood fame, Lorne Greene, gazed down upon one thousand invited guests. Just ushering in the distinguished guests involved a Guard of Honour, trumpets from the Governor General's Horse Guards, and pipers from the 48th Highlanders.

After the meal, Harry introduced each speaker with typical Foster ease, class and charm and the TV cameras whirled. Each dignitary brought words of encouragement to the Crusade, and Mrs. Kennedy's speech brought a standing ovation. The gift presented to her to remember the occasion was a painting of Mount Kennedy. Harry had arranged for the artist to be flown into the Yukon to do his sketches. This had been done in the early summer of 1965 when the mountain was first climbed by a team that included Robert F. Kennedy. Rose Kennedy was moved to tears by the appropriateness of the presentation.

The highlight of the evening, in an evening of highlights, was two surprise recorded messages which Harry had arranged. The first was from Elizabeth, the Queen Mother, accompanied by a slide showing her opening a children's school for the disabled. The second message came from Jean Vanier, son of Governor General and Mrs. Vanier and a famous humanitarian working with mentally disabled adults in France. As the young Vanier's portrait was projected onto the large screen, everybody heard his warm greeting to his parents and his moving tribute on behalf of disabled people everywhere.

Cultivating the political side of things in a seemingly unobtrusive way, Harry also showed a few photos of a young and athletic Lester Pearson and made the not-so-subtle inference that there was a connection between his sports career and his humanitarian efforts which resulted in a Nobel Prize. This was something to which Harry could relate.

He had already set the wheels in motion for government support for the Crusade, but he would pass up no opportunity to draw this fact to the attention of the public. These were all the sort of details that Harry relished. He believed they were vital in getting nation-wide attention for the Crusade. In this aspect he was right. *The Globe and Mail* columnist and friend Bruce West summarized the evening in an article entitled "Signs of Light":

It is a healthy sign, in a democracy, when the powerful are ready to reach down and offer a hand to the weak or less fortunate. Symbolizing this spirit as well as anything or anyone could was Harry E. (Red) Foster, the husky former athlete and now advertising man, who was chairman of the dinner and has long been one of the prime forces behind the efforts for the retarded child in Canada. Monday night's gala affair, for which he did most of the planning, was a resounding success and a fitting kick-off for a noble campaign.

The Centennial Crusade launching itself led to almost four years of intense effort by dedicated people all across Canada, and it raised nearly $17,000,000 when all the pledges were tabulated. It was truly a giant step forward in arousing government support and in confirming that the

Harry Foster carries the torch for the CARC to an Ottawa rally thanking the government for its support.

traditional public attitudes toward mental disabilities were being reversed. Harry himself attended the openings of most of the Crusade Projects as they materialized between 1966 and 1968. During Centennial Year, at the annual meeting of the provincial association in Ottawa, Harry organized a march on Parliament Hill. The 1960's was the era of marches and protests so another one, even for a good cause, would hardly be newsworthy. What caught the attention of the newspapers, however, was a typical Foster twist. The placards carried slogans of thanks to the Government for its help!

Harry could not have been prouder when the last of the Crusade projects, an employment training centre, opened in Toronto in 1971. This one was especially dear to his own heart because it was built on property he had donated himself on Birch Avenue, just a stone's throw from his own family home in the area where Jackie and his mother had walked. The establishment of this training facility was in itself a statement of a belief that the disabled could enjoy meaningful and productive participation in the life of the community if given the opportunity. Appropriately, it was named in Harry's honour by the Metropolitan Toronto Association in recognition of the work and financial support he had already given to the movement.

Signs of progress for the disabled were everywhere in the optimistic 1960's. "Patients" in institutions were now referred to as "residents." The term "retarded children" gave way to the "mentally retarded," and then to "handicapped" or "disabled" to encompass all people who suffered not from the "affliction" but from the "condition." The public school system in Ontario took over the schooling for disabled children in 1969, something which by then was seen as a right for disabled persons and not an act of charity. This move enabled the local associations to turn their attention to other needs such as sheltered workshops and group homes. Mentally handicapped people were firmly fixed on the path toward community-based care.

Harry was involved in all of the changes directly or indirectly, working as he did from the top down along with a host of volunteers who pushed from the bottom up. Harry specialized in big plans and followed them through with action. He challenged people, governments and corporations to become involved and to help make those big things happen. It came as no real surprise to anyone when in 1969, a grateful federal government bestowed upon him the Medal of Service of the Order of Canada.

One year earlier, his friends Lorne Greene and John Counsell had both been similarly honoured for outstanding service to the country. At the ceremony at Government House in 1969 and accepting awards of their own were more friends from the sporting world, including Russ Jackson from football, Jean Beliveau from hockey and Elaine Tanner from swimming. Harry was certainly in good company. Of course, he was enormously proud of his own achievement and the honour but even in accepting it, he did so on behalf of the thousands of parents who had fought the battles with him. Letters of congratulations poured in and Harry not only kept them all but responded to each and every one in the weeks after the ceremony. Typical of the

Harry E. Foster is awarded the Order of Canada in 1969 by Governor General Roland Michener for his years of work on behalf of disabled children.

praise which he received was a letter from Dr. Clare Bice, an old friend in the CARC who was then the President of the Royal Canadian Academy. He wrote:

> . . . *No one in this wonderful Canada deserves the Order of Canada more than you. Every leap ahead in Mental Retardation has been the product of your vision and dynamism and I think I'm one of the best informed to make that judgment. I'm so very very happy for you "Red." The seed I tried to sow year by year grew and matured because you had the good earth ready and they supplied the sunshine and rain. I am a lucky guy to have been part of the action. . . . We still have a long way to go but the road is less torturous now and we can apply more of our energy and abilities to creating, and less to convincing.*

Early in 1968, and a full year before Harry's Order of Canada Award, another event occurred that began innocently enough at a luncheon in Chicago, but ended up hatching yet another project, combining the creating and the convincing aspects of which Dr. Bice wrote. This was the Canadian Special Olympics, a project which would have far-reaching significance and one which would occupy the rest of Harry's days. It can only be seen as a logical progression in Harry Foster's life, one which in some ways fell into his lap but in other ways represents a torch which he consciously picked up and carried forward. It would, in fact, be the capstone of his career.

Chapter Nine
A Special Olympics

Like the capstone on an arch, the final crusade upon which Harry Foster would embark, would be built on strong foundations. For over a decade, both Canadian and American organizations for the mentally handicapped had been hard at work on many fronts. It was another of those fortunate combinations, this time involving cooperation across the Canada-USA border, that would add to the visibility and strength of the entire movement. Early in 1968, the Canadian Association for Retarded Children received welcome news from Washington. The association was to be honoured with a Leadership Award from the Joseph P. Kennedy Foundation in recognition of long-standing nation-wide cooperation and service to the mentally disabled. The award was to be presented in Chicago at a dinner celebration in April and as Honorary Chairman of the CARC, Harry Foster would accept it. For him, the invitation was a call to action. He saw in it another opportunity to promote the cause in high places and give some prominence to well-deserved Canadian efforts.

Not to be completely overshadowed by the glitter of the Kennedy Foundation's evening celebration, Harry decided to host a luncheon for Foundation representatives, the award recipients, the whole CARC contingent and the Canadian consular officials in Chicago. This idea of a VIP luncheon prior to an evening's gala dinner was not a new one. He had done the same thing in 1964 in New York when he coaxed Prime Minister Pearson to come and present a collection of press clippings to Sargent Shriver, the Executive Director of the Kennedy Foundation lauding the establishment of The Canadian John F. Kennedy Memorial Fund.

For the 1968 affair, Harry talked C.S. MacNaughton, the Treasurer of Ontario, and his friend Bill Davis, then the Minister of Education, into attending along with Stafford Smythe and Harold and Dorothy Ballard, whose executive jet was used for transportation. Harry organized Canadian entertainment, Canadian food, a flurry of appropriate speeches and the presentation of a cheque by Bill Davis on behalf of the Ontario Government for $185,000 for the Canadian Centennial Crusade projects. The cheque could just as easily been sent across town in Toronto by taxi, but the movement always came first and Harry was never short of an idea to promote it.

At the end of the luncheon, Harry made a point of speaking to Dr. Frank Hayden of the University of Western Ontario, a member of the Canadian group. Hayden had been doing some exciting research into physical fitness for the mentally handicapped. Harry was aware of this effort and was also aware of Hayden's work with the Kennedy Foundation in establishing special fitness programs for the mentally disabled in the United States. Harry said to Frank, "I hear that you have something going on in July that I might be interested in!" He was referring to the American Games for the Retarded. The two men talked only briefly, but that was the moment that Harry Foster was hooked on the possibility of Canadian participation. The dinner celebration that evening was indeed a great honour for the CARC and other Award winners, but Harry's mind was already leaping forward to a new horizon.

Frank Hayden had been building his credentials for almost a decade as an expert in the new field of physical fitness for mentally disabled children. His strength as a young Ph.D. candidate lay in research on fitness levels for various segments of the population, an area where reliable information was virtually non-existent. Part of his early work was in association with the ground breaking Canadian Air Force 5 BX fitness program which had already gained world-wide attention. In 1960, Hayden helped to establish a research program, sponsored by five Toronto Rotary Clubs, to measure and assess the physical fitness of mentally disabled children in the day schools operated by the Toronto Association.

After almost four years of pioneering effort, Hayden produced a manual in 1964 for teachers and parents entitled *Physical Fitness for the Mentally Retarded.* This was the first scientific study of its kind in the world and it showed clearly that the strength and endurance of these children could be substantially improved by physical activity. For its time, this was nothing short of revolutionary, and it constituted an assault on the then current notion that the disabled could not or should not be involved in sport.

The publication of Hayden's findings in 1964 coincided with the initial planning for the Canadian Centennial celebrations. Canadians everywhere were being urged to make suggestions for projects which would really get the country involved. This, of course, was part of the background for Harry Foster's Centennial Crusade. Hayden, for his part, made a proposal for a Centennial Crusade Project himself. He put forward a scheme of local fitness development programs introducing the mentally handicapped to competition. This was to be followed by province-wide games in 1966, and some sort of national games in 1967. Naturally enough these would be called the Centennial Games for the Mentally Retarded.

The Canadian Centennial Commission became extremely excited about the potential of the proposal, but the CARC showed little interest. Like Harry Foster, who paid little attention to Hayden's proposal at the time, the CARC's priorities were centered on the mammoth Crusade. Fortunately, and somewhat typically of many Canadian initiatives over the years, the Americans were attracted to the

Floor hockey was the first sport played by Canadian Special Olympians at the 1968 Games in Chicago.

idea. Specific enthusiasm came from Eunice Kennedy Shriver of the Kennedy Foundation who persuaded Hayden to come to Washington in 1965 to set up his program. He did so and eventually would devote more than six years to working with them at their Washington headquarters.

By 1967, after considerable ground work had been done at local levels in the United States, it was decided that they were ready for some sort of national track meet. The Foundation decided to wait, however, until July 1968 in order to capitalize on the excitement of the Olympics in Mexico City that year. Frank Hayden's logical suggestion to launch the games as the Special Olympics for the Retarded was eagerly adopted.

The possibility of Canadian participation at the July 1968 Games, was the subject of the brief conversation between Frank Hayden and Harry Foster at that Chicago luncheon in April. Frank suggested that Harry bring a floor hockey team back to Chicago to demonstrate an activity that had great potential as a fitness tool for the mentally disabled. Harry immediately accepted the invitation. Canadian participation would give the first American effort an international flavour and would also demonstrate more active support to the Kennedy Foundation. It might also be the beginning of a new set of programs for the Canadian movement which in turn would certainly be a boost for the local associations where physical fitness programs were clearly lagging behind those of their American counterparts.

Floor hockey is a team game that is easy to learn and fun to play, and it already had players at the Beverley Street School in Toronto. With less than three months to put all the details together, it was a logical decision to send a floor hockey team. Harry was at work on this decision even as the plane winged its way home from the Chicago Kennedy Foundation celebration.

One of the major difficulties Harry faced when he arrived home was the less than enthusiastic reception his idea received in Toronto. True, nobody's enthusiasm could match Harry's when he seized upon an idea, but there were also many concerns. At this the time, the schools for the mentally disabled were on the verge of being taken over by the government. This led to questions of jurisdiction and liability. Moreover, those directly involved with education for the mentally disabled were not particularly keen on sports programs at the time. There were some who feared that these children could not learn the rules sufficiently and some who worried that promoting competition and body

Members of the Canadian Special Olympics floor hockey team sport Toronto Maple Leaf sweaters as they march in the opening ceremonies parade 1969.

The four principal organizers of the Special Olympics in the United States and Canada watch a floor hockey game in Toronto in 1973. From left to right are Beverly Campbell of the Kennedy Foundation, Harry Foster, Eunice Kennedy Shriver, and Frank Hayden.

contact was potentially setting up these children for more losing situations. Others thought that journeys by aeroplane and living in modern hotels simply might be too overwhelming! Harry addressed these concerns as best he could, but he knew that only a real live test would convince the doubters.

The group that went to Chicago's Soldier's Memorial Field in July was truly a Harry Foster creation, with a little help from his friends. Financial sponsorship came through the Foster Foundation. Harold Ballard himself joined the group and provided blue and white Toronto Maple Leaf uniforms; he also flew the Canadian press corps to Chicago and back at his expense. Maple Leaf Captain George Armstrong volunteered to be the coach and Stan Mikita of the Chicago Black Hawks was recruited to guide a Chicago-based team. The competition itself took place on a plywood floor in the middle of the track at Soldier Field. The game, which ended in a tie, was described as exciting for both the players and the crowd alike. There was plenty of body-checking and also excellent sportsmanship. These children were proving that they could learn. They could laugh and have fun, and they could even win or lose gracefully — if only they were given a chance. As predicted, these youngsters displayed a spirit of courage and determination that would help to overcome so many of the labels and obstacles that the world had imposed upon them for so long.

There is no question that it was a tremendously emotional moment for Harry when the Canadian floor hockey team marched in accompanied by Canadian flags and a marching band. Though there were less than one thousand American competitors, one tiny Canadian team, and a mere handful of spectators in the stands to cheer them all on, there were not many dry eyes among them when Eunice Shriver led the assembled in the Special Olympics oath: "Let me win, but if I cannot win, let me be brave in the attempt." The American Special Olympics program had marked its beginnings. For Canada, the experience was like a sown seed. With Harry Foster holding the watering can, it was almost inevitable that the seed would sprout.

It was only a matter days after the team's return from the successful Chicago experience that Harry set himself and the Foster Foundation on the path towards the first Canadian Special Olympics. These were immediately scheduled for Toronto for June 1969. Harry was determined not only that these games should come to Canada, but also, after some positive encouragement from Frank Hayden, that his Foundation should be the means of making it all happen. He was convinced that there were enormous potential benefits for the mentally disabled, and he was certain that the games were a perfect vehicle for raising wide public awareness.

Any sports connection always rang bells in Harry's fertile mind. In his own past, sports had brought him numerous opportunities to have fun and to win and they appealed on a level that everyone could understand. The Special Olympics concept would preserve all of this and would give Harry a new opportunity to lead the movement in a new direction. There would be no shortage of challenges in the months ahead, but thinking and planning on a

Harry greets Rose Kennedy at the Toronto International Airport as she arrives for the Special Olympics in 1969.

grand scale and facing problems head on was a deeply established Foster characteristic.

Aside from Harry's dogged determination to make the games a show piece for the movement for the mentally handicapped, the key to their success lay in their endorsement by prominent public figures. In securing such support, Harry was a master strategist. Through Harold Ballard, Harry got a formal introduction to Clarence Campbell, the President of the National Hockey League, and this connection allowed Harry to obtain the co-operation of all twelve National Hockey League teams. Campbell even agreed to be the Honorary Chairman of the games. Each of his clubs agreed to sponsor a floor hockey team from their city, and that support would include a player/coach, uniforms, food and transportation. This was the first major recognition of the Special Olympics by an organized group of professional athletes, and it became the springboard for many heart-warming connections between individual superstars and handicapped children. Harold Ballard himself not only donated Maple Leaf Gardens but also promised the plywood for the playing surfaces and the dressing rooms for each team to sleep in during the tournament. He would turn the Gardens into a "hockey village" complete with catered food services.

With official NHL support in place by late fall in 1968, Harry went to work to secure the presence of Mrs. Rose Kennedy. Working through her daughter, Eunice Shriver, and the Kennedy Foundation, Harry sought to continue his warm and genuine friendship with Rose which had begun at the time of the launching of the Centennial Crusade in 1965. Their personal relationship stemmed both from their well-known work on behalf of the mentally disabled and from the fact that the Kennedy's mentally disabled daughter, Rosemary, reminded Red so much of his own brother Jackie. Rose and Red also shared a lively Irish heritage and strong religious faith. Here was an opportunity to highlight a prominent American who could bring a message of hope to parents. Rose accepted Red's invitation without hesitation exactly the way Red himself would have seen it — a chance to talk about mental disabilities. "I can speak to parents who are overwrought, baffled about what to do with their children," she said. "I understand the cross they bear and can speak from the heart and comfort them." Red understood this completely.

With Mrs. Kennedy's presence guaranteed, Harry launched a personal campaign for corporate sponsors and volunteers that was truly remarkable. The Royal York Hotel promised its vice-regal suite for Mrs. Kennedy and her entourage, and John Bassett Sr. lent his Lear jet to transport them all from Hyannis Port, Massachusetts. Canadian Kodak supplied all of the movie film, Canada Dry donated thousands of drinks, and the radio stations provided hundreds of announcements on the air prior to the games. The paper work for the swimming and track programs was worked out for the athletes and a veritable army of volunteers, the "meeters, greeters, and huggers," was put into place in the weeks before the games.

On June 11, 1969, over 1400 young people with their chaperones descended on Toronto for the first Canadian Special Olympics. The two days of games that followed at the Jim Vipond Pool, the CNE stadium and at Maple Leaf Gardens were a resounding success. As usual, the marchpast of the athletes and the lighting of the flame provided the highlights. They were powerfully emotional moments for the spectators, the honourary coaches marching with the athletes, and the distinguished guests alike. Harry was also very emotional on these occasions and his tears were ones of pure joy at seeing the kids trying so hard. Lotta Dempsey of *The Toronto Star* wrote:

People clapped and cheered and there was a pride among them; and one felt the wall of distance between the retarded and so many who did not know or understand them before, melting away. There was a sudden bond among us all, celebrating life.

As Harry had so often pointed out in the past, this is what the movement for the disabled was all about. In a note to Rose Kennedy just before the games, he had shared his own sense of pride by noting that:

If my late parents, who during their lifetimes looked after my retarded and blind brother, were alive today and were told that 10 plane loads of retarded children would be flying from 10 major cities in the United States to take part in Special Olympic Games in a foreign country, they would be dumbfounded. It would be equally hard for them to believe that 1,400 children from 49 cities and towns in Canada would also be participating in these games.

Harry Foster, Rose Kennedy, and Clarence Campbell watch the opening ceremonies of the Special Olympics held in Toronto in 1969.

The Special Olympics in Canada were launched with a fanfare of hype and publicity that kept Toronto buzzing all week. The games were filled with moments of determination and courage from all the athletes. There was thunderous cheering for the participants in some races who struggled across the finish lines in last place, and for those who stopped before the end of their event to wait for their friends to catch up. There were thrilling moments for the athletes themselves when they heard the bands playing and parents and friends cheering just for them, for the first time in their lives. Receiving individual attention from the many sports celebrities who Red had coaxed into acting as honorary coaches awakened strong emotions for athletes and celebrities alike.

Mrs. Kennedy was a star in her own genuine and enthusiastic way, and she exhausted herself shouting and cheering with Red and everyone else. There were frustrating moments for the hundreds of volunteers who struggled with the mountains of paper but these frustrations always seemed to vanish when they could hug the participants and share the joy that the athletes demonstrated so easily. And there was an extra special moment for Harry too when, as master of ceremonies, he was praising the work of the Kennedy family noting that ". . . in Canada we don't have a President Kennedy. . ." Mrs. Kennedy leaned over to the microphone and said, "Well, in Canada, you DO have a 'Red' Foster!"

It was the spirit of giving and fun that galvanized the games in those June days and it was that spirit which laid the

Rose Kennedy joins in the fun at the Canadian Special Olympics in Toronto in 1969.

solid foundation for more. The games took root remarkably quickly in the fabric of the lives of the mentally handicapped in Canada as well as in Harry's own mind. There was a Second International Games in Chicago in 1970 after a series of games in various provinces, and a second Canadian games in 1971 in Toronto with Prime Minister Pierre Elliot Trudeau and Ontario Premier Bill Davis as the featured guests. In fact, games have been held somewhere every year thereafter, and a quarter of a century later they continue as an important organizational outlet for the personal development of those with mental handicaps. The Special Olympics still contain those highly charged emotional moments, and they still attract hundreds of volunteers many of whom switch hats on a daily basis, leaving aside for a moment their duties elsewhere.

The games of the Special Olympics could never have been successful without the army of volunteers working with individuals behind the scenes at the grass roots levels and Harry always heaped praise on their efforts, churning

out an endless stream of thank-you notes. He was always more proficient, however, in working from the top down and he was never shy about phoning the leading professional athletes of the day to lend a hand. His own athletic background, his connections with Harold Ballard of the Toronto Maple Leafs, and his prominent role in the Sports Hall of Fame made the contacts easier.

Among the many prominent athletes who made a difference to so many Special Olympians were Bryan Watson, Johnny Bower, Maurice Richard, Jean Beliveau and former Maple Leaf captains George Armstrong and Darryl Sittler. Typical among that group is former Maple Leaf and Calgary Flame star Lanny McDonald whose arm Harry had first twisted to do a commercial for the Special Olympics. Harry had needed Lanny on a particular Monday for the filming and as Lanny later stated, "With Red, it didn't matter 'when' as long as 'when' was 'now'."[4] The commercial was filmed, of course, and McDonald's association with the organization continued for more than twenty years.

Harry had always seen the athletic stars of the day as important motivators of favourable public opinion and as excellent role models for children. From the success of his Crown Brand Christmas Ice Carnivals in the late 1930's through to the Special Olympics, his exploitation of the prominence of leading sporting figures had created the win-win programs which were his trademark. A contact here and a phone call there usually brought the desired results. By the mid 1970's, however, the task of securing the big names was becoming more and more difficult as most players were beginning to work under complex endorsement contracts and with agents who controlled their availability. Harry admitted being very discouraged at times over this problem but he was never one to let any set-back hold him down for long. He came to cherish the contacts he had made even more and to work harder to come up with other ideas that would keep the Special Olympics in the public eye.

---

[4] Lanny McDonald with Steve Simmons, *Lanny* (Toronto: McGraw-Hill, 1987), p. 153.

Prime Minister Pierre Elliot Trudeau is introduced by Harry Foster to a floor hockey team at the second Canadian Special Olympics held in Toronto in 1971.

Before the 1975 International Games in Mount Pleasant, Michigan, Harry had conceived the idea of pre-games training camps. For the 1975 camp, the venue he selected was his old school, Ridley College in St. Catharines. This idea was designed partly to ensure that there would be a good showing by the Canadian group in Michigan and also for the added opportunity it would give to highlight the Canadian organizational work and training efforts. The athletes were given opportunities to get to know one another and there were clinics in the fundamentals of all the events and especially in floor hockey, the activity which

Harry was most closely attached himself. Many nostalgic memories must have flooded his mind as he practised with the boys at the very site of his own 1920's boyhood hockey experiences.

Part of the fun which was built into the training camp days was a bus tour scheduled for nearby Niagara Falls. For some reason, Harry was anxious that the athletes see this great tourist attraction from the American side but he did not want to keep the athletes waiting in the heat in a potential bottleneck at the border crossing. His solution — a police escort over and back — to impress the authorities

Ontario Premier William Davis helps Harry carry the banner at the 1971 Canadian Special Olympics at Ontario Place.

with the importance of the group! How he arranged this is not known, but it is very typical of his fancy for turning any event into a bit of a show. Typically, also, the press and film coverage at the school was exhaustive even before the athletes again ventured across the border to Michigan. Toward the end of the camp, the summer temperatures were threatening to make the nine-hour bus ride unbearable. As a solution, Harry simply decided to charter a jet to transport the whole company.

In 1977, Appleby College in Red's new home town of Oakville was the site for the Invitational Special Olympic Games which were slated for June. These games would be attended only by Ontario athletes and as the first province-wide competition of its kind, they were intended to demonstrate what other provinces could also do in terms of planning and staging games of their own. The idea of using Appleby College was Red's and was a result of the successful experience at Ridley College in 1975. In the late winter, the requests for the time and the use of the school's facilities came across the Appleby Headmaster's desk, and at the first planning meeting for the games, he expressed some objections to Harry's assumption that the school would automatically throw open its gates for the Special Olympians.

Harry plays a little pick-up floor hockey with some Special Olympic athletes at Ridley College in 1975.

In typical Foster fashion, Harry made a few discreet phone calls to key Appleby Board members. At the next planning meeting, there was "no problem"! When Red was pushing, it was very difficult for anyone to say "no" to his enthusiasm, his persuasiveness, and his dynamic personality. As the planning stages neared completion, another and more serious problem emerged. A local diphtheria case was uncovered and the Health authorities recommended cancellation of the entire effort. True to his ability to rebound in the face of disappointment, Harry simply rescheduled the whole affair for August.

Demonstrating his knack for creating his own luck, Harry set the August date to coincide with the induction of athletes into Canada's Sports Hall of Fame. Using his influence as Chairman of that institution and as Honorary Chairman of the Special Olympics as well, he talked most of the inductees into lending their support by joining the marchpasts with the Special Olympians and generally helping out. The change in date also enabled the famous 155-member Burlington Teen Tour Band to lend their

Harry Foster presents the Lou Marsh trophy to Athlete of the Year, Guy Lafleur, in front of a picture which shows Guy with his Special Olympics floor hockey team.

musical support and add some of the showbiz elements which Harry always believed were critical to the overall public impact. As usual, Harry refused to take any credit for his work behind the scenes but, also as usual, the games' organization took on a team approach which spread out both the work and the costs. He got the NHL to sponsor the floor hockey teams again and Harold Ballard to supply the plywood for the rink floors. His connections with the Royal Bank covered the costs of the medals and ribbons, and Wintario agreed to pick up many of the miscellaneous

Harry Foster walks with Lanny McDonald, Ontario Lieutenant Governor John Black Aird and a Special Olympic athlete at the Lieutenant Governor's reception during the 1982 Canadian Special Olympic Games.

expenses.

The games began on Friday the 26th with Oakville's mayor lighting the torch at the town hall. It was carried to Appleby by Special Olympians and it burned symbolically during the games and was extinguished on Sunday morning after a mammoth closing ceremony which featured John Rae, the Canadian Frisbee Champion and his dog. In all, over 400 athletes had participated and the games marked another tremendous boost for the concept of sports for the mentally handicapped. Their success, as in the past, was cemented by the choice of venue, the celebrities who took part, the host of volunteers who gave their time, and the constant flow of press releases which Harry made sure

followed every winning performance. Harry was not only the master of detail, he was highly skilled in using the press to publicize the philosophy of the games. What he would tell the reporters in a seemingly off-hand and spontaneous manner, would be incorporated in their stories. "Look at all the happiness — the beautiful faces," he said to one of them after the opening ceremonies. "These kids have been stuck behind the big high fences too long . . . [they] have been losers all their lives, and now everyone is a winner . . . we are working to have the mentally retarded function to their greatest level." Before the books were closed on the Appleby experience, plans were set in motion for the next games in Saskatchewan in 1978.

Harry at the Opening Ceremonies of the 1977 Canadian Special Olympic Games at Appleby College in Oakville.

In spite of its general success, the evolution of the Special Olympics program in the 1970's was not without its growing pains. The Foster Foundation could not shoulder the entire cost of the operation, so fund-raising continued to occupy much of Harry's energies. There was also a conflict of opinion with the CARC and with some of the dedicated workers in the field of mental disabilities. Some saw the Special Olympics as actually running contrary to their philosophy of normalization, and others sometimes questioned Harry's all-out, single-minded and take-charge methods of operation.

Harry supported the goal of integrating the mentally handicapped in the normal flow of everyday life, but how clearly he really understood the concept remains an open question. At worst, he reverted many times to seeing the mentally disabled like his brother, as children who would never grow up. At best, he saw the achievement of the goal of integration much farther down the road than some were ready to admit.

In the meantime, and as a product of his own athletic background, he believed with a passion that there was an important role for the Special Olympics to play in building the confidence and self-esteem so important to the development of the participants. Harry's apparent preoccupation with the Special Olympics concept caused some people real concern, the fear being that the general movement for the mentally disabled would lose Harry as a major benefactor.

If others outside the organization had concerns about Harry, Harry also had concerns of his own. He was often frustrated with what he considered a lack of vision in some quarters and the slowness with which some people came to realize that physical training, exercise and competition were truly beneficial to those with developmental handicaps. He was saddened, too, with the lack of interest that the Americans in particular showed for his beloved floor hockey. He dreamed of a league of floor hockey players across the continent, backed by the National Hockey League, as an integral part of the Special Olympics. While the NHL support continues to this day, and floor hockey is still an important part of the recreation programs across the country, Harry's dream never materialized.

Somewhat sadly in 1974, there was a parting of the ways between the Canadian Association for Retarded Children and the Canadian Special Olympics which was officially

The satisfaction of having a lifetime's achievement on behalf of disabled people recognized is evident on the face of Harry Foster as he receives an honorary doctorate degree from the University of Western Ontario in 1979.

chartered as a separate organization in November of that year. In hindsight, however, the separation can be seen as a benefit to both organizations. There was (and is) enough work for everyone, with thousands of mentally handicapped people still to be helped in so many different ways by different organizations.

As the Canadian Special Olympics program went through its growing pains, Harry put a tremendous amount of his energy into its organization. As predicted by some, the Foster Foundation did become more selective in its assist-

ance, concentrating more and more on Special Olympics activities, but Harry never lost sight of the general goals for which everyone in the movement had worked for so long. He did not reduce his efforts in promoting full public acceptance of the mentally handicapped. His personal commitment continued; the way his brother had lived out his life would not be the fate of those who came after him.

Nor was Harry's involvement with mentally disabled people restricted to sports. Any opportunity to speak or act for the movement appealed to his interest. In 1974, he was an excited participant in an expedition to Canterbury in England to celebrate Easter in a unique way. This trip for over one hundred mentally disabled adults was financed through fund-raising drives, by a federal government grant and by the travellers themselves. The whole idea was not Harry's this time, but was conceived and arranged by his friends Ann and Steve Newroth who ran the Daybreak Hostel in Richmond Hill, just north of Toronto, which was associated in turn with the *L'Arche* residence movement in France founded and guided by Jean Vanier. Harry had tremendous respect for Vanier's work which was a product of the optimistic 1960's and of Vanier's intense Christian commitment. The chance to see him again in action was an opportunity he could not resist. "We're getting these people out from behind the fences," Harry said using his well-worn expression as they were leaving Toronto, and added, "Why shouldn't the retarded enjoy vacation trips and broaden their horizons like everyone else?"

Whose horizons were actually broadened by this excursion is an interesting question. That Easter service in the 11th century cathedral affected everyone. The Canadian pilgrims sat in the choir stalls while the Archbishop of Canterbury, Michael Ramsey, conducted the service. They placed gifts of traditional eggs and bread on the altar and a couple of boys even donated their Toronto Maple Leaf sweaters which had been presented by Harry a few hours earlier — a good will parting gift in bulk from Harold Ballard! When the service ended, the pilgrims, including Harry and the seventy-year-old Archbishop, moved down the aisles ringing bells in the medieval tradition and singing. They then formed a long circling snake dance in front of the church which lasted for nearly half an hour. This unique performance drew criticism from some of the locals, but in the words of Canon Donald Allchin of the cathedral, the real joy of Easter which came through in the music of the disabled was "the best thing that happened in the cathedral in about 500 years!" Harry too was thoroughly caught up in the emotion of the day. In one of his reports telephoned to the Toronto press, he noted that the outlook of the people and their joy and happiness caused one to "soon stop your bellyaching about your own problems and make you realize how damn lucky you are." During the second week of the trip, everyone trooped over to France to visit the *L'Arche* communities and Harry took the opportunity to promote interest in floor hockey in France and to cultivate his dream of making the Special Olympics even more international.

Harry had to return to Canada a few days earlier than the rest. Putting his advanced arrival in Toronto to good use, he planned a big news conference for the airport to greet the return of the pilgrims. Half way across the Atlantic on the pilgrims' flight home, however, the pilots were informed that a strike of the fire services at the Toronto airport would necessitate their landing in New York with a ten-hour bus ride to get them back to Toronto. One can imagine their anguish! The trip had been exhausting and some of the participants were running low on their medications. When Harry heard the news back in Toronto, he was on two phones at once. What started as an ordinary plane ride suddenly became a mercy flight. The plane did land in Toronto. By himself, he had struck a three hour special deal with the fire fighter's union! The press conference took place as planned, the disabled got the coverage and, in typical Foster style, the fire fighters got the credit.

Another project which made Harry enormously proud blossomed in 1977 after five years of effort. The idea for this one was born in 1973 when Harry was in the Oakville hospital recovering from minor surgery. One night during his short stay, he heard the cries of a young man in a nearby ward who was receiving no attention from the duty nurses. Harry got out of bed and discovered that the lad was mentally disabled and that the nurses were too frightened to go near him. Harry consoled the patient and helped him through the night, but this incident sparked the idea for longer range assistance. A set of four films for nurses was eventually produced by experts. The films stressed the social and educational implications of mental disabilities, teaching the professionals how to better cope with persons with this condition. Harry secured the support of the Atkinson Charitable Foundation to fund most of the project, thus turning another dream into a reality. When Harry saw the films for the first time, there were more tears of joy as they reminded him so much of the day more than twenty years before when he had faced the camera himself in the ten minute appeal of *The Lady on My Street.*

By 1980, Harry, then 75 years old, began to show signs of slowing down. He developed nagging problems with ulcers which must have made clear to him that the frantic pace of a lifetime could not continue forever. As one can imagine, Harry was not a very good patient when it came to following his doctor's advice on the treatment for the ulcers. He did continue his life-long habit of a swim or a jog almost every day well into the 1980's, although these became shorter and less frequent as time wore on.

No doubt by 1980, Harry could have looked back, if he had wanted to, with considerable satisfaction on a lifetime of effort in building both a successful advertising enterprise and strong organizations to benefit Canada's mentally handicapped citizens. By this time there was a solid group of directors both in the Foundation he had established and in the Special Olympics which he had founded. As in his advertising agency in the early 1970's, there were those who had ably taken over the work he had begun. The old workaholic approach to things was no longer really appropriate.

Harry, however, did not look back very often. There were still games and floor hockey tournaments to attend. The flow of ideas and plans from his Special Olympics office at 40 St. Clair Avenue during these years confirm that Harry continued only to look forward. Any reflection that he permitted on his life was done by other people and by organizations that honoured him in the steady stream of tributes which marked the early 1980's. As so many reflected upon the depth of the contributions he had made in so many areas over a lifetime, he could only be enormously pleased although he never rested content.

His Honorary Doctorate in 1979, for instance, from the University of Western Ontario was awarded largely in recognition of his humanitarian service and social conscience. Harry had always had an affinity for people with degrees and to have one of his own at last was a tremendous thrill for him; but he was also filled with an inner pride knowing that all of his work had been done without formal university training. In so many ways, the school of service to others had been his greatest teacher and his greatest reward.

The Royal Bank Award in 1981 for his dedication to the mentally disabled was one which he had actually anticipated for a number of years, and its cash value of $50,000 had been earmarked many times over for the work of the Foundation. His induction as a builder into Canada's Sports Hall of Fame in 1984 brought his life full circle, from the sporting champion in his early years to a champion of service to all sports at the end. What was honoured was a fierce competitive spirit that always played by the rules and which had had so many positive spinoffs in areas other than sports. Harry accepted all of the honours bestowed in these last years with dignity and grace, and his acceptance speeches continued to combine humour and the ever present plug for mentally disabled children.

In sharing his strength and energy with those who were weaker and in need of help, Harry had touched the lives of thousands of people. He had demonstrated time and again that the mentally handicapped were real people with real needs. For parents, having a mentally disabled child was no longer a cause for shame. The mentally handicapped themselves had been given the chance to demonstrate to everyone the true meaning of sportsmanship, character and courage.

Harry had actively demonstrated a genuine faith in God, a faith in himself and a faith in others, as he had successfully challenged people to think and act on higher levels than they would ever have imagined possible. He had demonstrated how to seize the moment, how to make big things really happen. There was, too, a noble quality about everything he did, in honouring his parents, in his love for his brother, in his devotion to his wife and, especially, in his concern for the disadvantaged. He got people to share the loving nature of the less fortunate and to experience how able they were in drawing out the goodness in everyone. These things were all recognized in a dozen honours and testimonials in the early 1980's.

One Sunday, late in 1984, the ulcers which had long plagued him caused his collapse in church. Maintaining his humour even as he was being carried out, he lamented the fact that the collection had already been taken! His condition was serious, however, and he was sent to the hospital in Oakville and soon after transferred to Toronto where he was placed in intensive care. There he admitted that this was the toughest fight of his life, the one for life itself. Gradually, in January, his kidneys closed down and his heart weakened. His last days were uncomfortable but his greatest concern was that Jimmie, his wife, would be looked after. His last fight was one which he was fated to lose, but when we consider how his life was spent, that loss was surely a rarity in a long series of win-win situations. He himself was a winner in the world of things that really matter, and that world was made a bit better for having experienced him. On January 18, 1985, two months short of his 80th birthday, the light went out on Harry "Red" Foster, a very special Canadian indeed.

Bibliography

Pulling together the myriad of bits and pieces that constitute the record of the life of any individual is always a challenge. Interpreting those fragments left by a man such as Harry E. Foster against the backdrop of the time in which he lived only adds to that challenge. In the end, it is up to the reader to judge how complete the record is and how well the story has been told. Because Harry's life involved so many distinct parts, I have chosen to divide the bibliography into compartments that may help any reader who would like further information on a particular aspect.

The three major Toronto newspapers were perhaps the best sources for some of the details of many of Harry's activities in the 1920's and 1930's. In the realm of sports in particular, his name and his teams appeared often. His friends, sports columnists Lou Marsh and Ted Reeve, painted a most detailed picture of the sporting scene in those decades and their columns provide fascinating reading for anyone with the patience to crank through the reels of microfilm. The same may be said about the unindexed issues of *Marketing* magazine which record the advertising activities of the Foster agency.

The best source of information on the early days of Canadian radio is Bill McNeil and Morris Wolfe's *Signing On: The Birth of Radio in Canada*. This work records the experiences of many of Canada's radio pioneers and is accompanied by many fine photographs. Similarly, T.J. Allard's *Straight Up: Private Broadcasting in Canada: 1918-1958*, is the only book which deals with the unique problems of private broadcasting. Worth reading too for the sake of pure nostalgia is J. Fred MacDonald's *Don't Touch That Dial! Radio Programming in American Life*. This is a compendium of the programs that dominated the American air waves and consequently those in Canada as well. There is as yet no Canadian companion volume.

As for the history of specific Canadian businesses, much historical work remains to be done. There are some good business histories already on the market and historian Duncan McDowall's *Quick to the Frontier* may well set the standard for some time. His is a history of the Royal Bank, one of Harry's clients for some years. Too often the records of firms get destroyed over the years because storage space costs money and when an enterprise folds, its records are usually house cleaned. This happened in the case of the Foster Advertising Agency.

Social history is currently a burgeoning field in Canadian studies and the histories of the growth of a variety of movements for human betterment are receiving much wider attention now than they did in the past. Dr. Mary Tremblay of McMaster University, for instance, is engaged in some pioneering investigations of the Canadian Paraplegic Association. A history of the beginnings of the whole movement for the mentally disabled has yet to be undertaken although Betty Anglin and June Braaten's *Twenty-Five Years of Growing Together: A History of the Ontario Association for the Mentally Retarded*, is an excellent beginning in this area.

The quotations from newspaper sources which I have used are all acknowledged in the text. Those made by Harry Foster originate in the papers of the Harry E. Foster Collection in the Public Archives of Canada and I would be happy to furnish the exact location for each of them for any interested reader. Harry's papers are now with the Manuscript Division, the 16mm films are with the Photographic Division and the tape recordings are housed in the Sound Division. A veritable truckload of material was removed from Harry's Oakville basement in 1993 all eventually to became part of the Harry E. Foster Collection in Ottawa.

Finally, and as a small step in providing some insight into the work of a colourful Canadian who did play a prominent role in Canada's sporting history, her business history and in the history of the movement on behalf of the mentally disabled, I relied heavily upon the reminiscences of people who knew Harry Foster in one way or another over his lifetime. I conducted all of the interviews myself. While most were in the Toronto area, I did enjoy a trip to Washington and two trips to Florida in the process. Eventually, I hope to make the pertinent material available to the Public Archives. Listed below are those who were kind enough to share their memories of Harry with me:

Don Allan, Larry Anas, Gerald and Betty Anglin, George Armstrong, Bill Ballard, John Black, Al Bolin, Roy Bonisteel, Norman Bosworth, Henry Botchford, Dr. Harry Botterell, Ab Box, R.A. Bradley, Beverly Campbell, Bob Cauley, Arthur Collins, Chris Commins, Frank Coy, Lynn Greer (Crawford), Doreen Crystal, Senator Keith Davey, Rev. Ian Dingwall, Wentworth Dowell, Angela and Alex Dobosi, Susan Edwards, Kathy Frazee, Rowland Frazee, Rev. Gordon George, Owen Greening, Tibor Gregor, Elizabeth Gordon, Adam Griffith, John Haddad, Ted Harper, Martha Harron, Frank Hayden, Sam Heaman, Bill Hearn, Denis Jotcham, Ross Knechtel, Ruth Krieger, Allen Lamport, Bob Little, Alex MacKay, George MacKinnon, Lou MacPherson, Donald C. Masters, John Maw, Neil McKenty, Joe McNulty, Dominic Morabito, Steve and Ann Newroth, Bill Orrett, H. J. Packard, Emma Mae Parker, Evelyn Reeder, Joe Reeve, Dr. Terry Riley, Linda Rosier, Frank Selke Jr., Bob Shaw, Sam Shefsky, Barry Singer, Harry Slemin, Robert E. Stanley, Nancy Stone, Dolly Tarshis, Howard Tate, Lorraine Taylor, Fred Tilley, Mary Tremblay, Bryan Vaughan, Joan Vitalis, Ann Webber, Bill Whitehead, Harold Wilson, John Withrow, and George Young.

CANADA, TORONTO, RIDLEY COLLEGE

Beattie, Kim. *Ridley: The Story of a School.* St. Catharines: Ridley College, 1963.

Berton, Pierre. *The Dionne Years: A Thirties Melodrama.* Toronto: McClelland & Stewart, 1977.

Granatstein, J.L. Abella, Irving M., Bercuson, David J., Brown, R.Craig, Neatby, H. Blair. *Twentieth Century Canada.* Toronto: McGraw-Hill Ryerson Ltd., 1983.

Gzowski, Peter. *A Sense of Tradition: An Album of Ridley College Memories, 1889-1989.* St. Catharines: Ridley College, 1988.

Kilbourn, William. *Intimate Grandeur: One Hundred Years at Massey Hall.* Toronto: Stoddart, 1993.

West, Bruce. *Toronto.* Toronto: Doubleday Canada Ltd., 1967.

SPORTS

Conacher, Charlie and Trent G. Frayne. "Me and My Family." *Macleans*, Vol.70, March 2, 1957, pp. 9-11.

Frayne, Trent. *The Queen's Plate.* Toronto: McClelland & Stewart, 1989.

Harper, Ted. *Six Days of Madness.* Stroud, Ontario: Pacesetter Press, 1993.

Houston, William. *Ballard.* Toronto: Summerhill Press, 1984.

McDonald, Lanny with Steve Simmons. *Lanny.* Toronto: McGraw-Hill Ryerson Ltd., 1987.

McFarlane, Brian. *50 Years of Hockey, 1917-1967.* Toronto: Pagurian Press, 1967.

Selke, Frank with H. Gordon Green. *Behind the Cheering.* Toronto: McClelland & Stewart, 1962.

Sullivan, Jack. *The Grey Cup Story: The Dramatic History Of Football's Most Coveted Award.* Toronto: Pagurian Press, 1974.

Wilson, Harold. *Boats Unlimited.* Erin, Ontario: The Boston Mills Press, 1990.

Wise, S.F. and Douglas Fisher. *Canada's Sporting Heroes.* Don Mills: General Publishing Co., 1974.

RADIO

Aitken, Kate. *Making Your Living Is Fun.* Toronto: Longmans, Green & Co., 1959.

Allard, T.J. *Straight Up: Private Broadcasting in Canada: 1918-1958.* Ottawa: Heritage House Publishers, 1979.

Barris, Alex. *The Pierce-Arrow Showroom is Leaking: An Insider's View of the C.B.C.* Toronto: The Ryerson Press, 1969.

CBC, "The CBC is 50." Special Anniversary Issue. *Radio Guide,* November, 1986.

Drainie, Bronwyn. *Living the Part: John Drainie and the Dilemma of Canadian Stardom.* Toronto: Macmillan of Canada, 1988.

Dunning, John. *Tune in Yesterday: The Ultimate Encyclopedia of Old-Time Radio, 1935-1976.* Englewood Cliffs: Prentice-Hall, Inc., 1976.

Harron, Martha. *Don Harron: A Parent Contradiction.* Toronto: Collins, 1988.

Jack, Donald. *Sinc, Betty and the Morning Man.* Toronto: Macmillan of Canada, 1977.

MacDonald, J. Fred. *Don't Touch That Dial! Radio Programming in American Life, 1920-1960.* Chicago: Nelson-Hall, 1979.

McNeil, Bill and Morris Wolfe. *Signing On: The Birth of Radio in Canada.* Toronto: Doubleday Canada, 1982.

Packard, Frank L. *The Adventures of Jimmie Dale.* Toronto: The Copp Clark Co. Ltd., 1917.

Peers, Frank W. *The Politics of Broadcasting: 1920-1951.* Toronto: University of Toronto Press, 1969.

Roger, Ian. *Radio Drama.* London: The Macmillan Press, 1982.

Sinclair, Gordon. *Will The Real Gordon Sinclair Please Stand Up.* Toronto: McClelland & Stewart, 1966.

— *Will The Real Gordon Sinclair Please Sit Down.* Toronto: McClelland & Stewart, 1975.

Stewart, Sandy. *A Pictorial History of Radio in Canada.* Toronto: Gage Publishing Ltd., 1975.

— *From Coast to Coast: A Personal History of Radio in Canada.* Toronto: CBC Enterprises, 1985.

Troyer, Warner. *The Sound and the Fury: An Anecdotal History of Canadian Broadcasting.* Rexdale: John Wiley and Sons, 1980.

Twomey, John E. *Canadian Broadcasting History: Resources in English.* Toronto: Ryerson Polytechnical Institute, 1978.

Weir, E. Austin. *The Struggle for National Broadcasting in Canada.* Toronto: McClelland & Stewart, 1965.

Young, Scott. *Gordon Sinclair: A Life. . . And Then Some.* Toronto: Macmillan of Canada, 1987.

ADVERTISING AND BUSINESS

Amys, John H. *The Albany.* Toronto: Yorkminster Publishing Ltd., 1981.

Edmonds, Elizabeth. "The True Blue Red." *Marketing,* January 25, 1971. p. 3.

— "Foster Keeps His Promise." *Marketing,* April 30, 1973, p. 1.

Flohill, R. "Spotlight on Red Foster." *Sales Promotion,* February-March, 1966, p. 21.

Kieran, J.W. "Close-Up on Red Foster." *Canadian Television & Motion Picture Review,* February, 1955, p. 8.

MacKinnon, George. "The Double Life of Harry Red Foster." *Executive,* September, 1969, p. 7.

Stephenson, H.E. and C. McNaught. *The Story of Advertising in Canada: A Chronicle of Fifty Years.* Toronto: Ryerson Press, 1940.

MENTAL HANDICAPS

Anglin, Betty and June Braaten. *Twenty-Five Years of Growing Together: A History of the Ontario Association for the Mentally Retarded.* Toronto: Canadian Association for the Mentally Retarded, 1978.

Berquist, L. "A Visit with the Indomitable Rose Kennedy." *Look,* Vol. 32, November 26, 1968, pp. 25-34.

Katz, Sidney. "The Amazing Career of Clare Hincks." *Macleans,* Vol. 67, August 1, 1954, pp. 10-11.

Simmons, Harvey G. *From Asylum to Welfare.* Toronto: National Institute for Mental Retardation.

Spink, Kathryn. *Jean Vanier and l'Arche: A Communion of Love.* New York, The Crossroad Publishing Co., 1990.

Vanier, Jean. *A Network of Friends: The Letters of Jean Vanier to the Friends and Communities of L'Arche. Vol. 1, 1964-1973.* Ed. John Sumarah. Hantsport, Nova Scotia: Lancelot Press Ltd., 1992.

PHOTO CREDITS

The Harry E. Foster Collection, National Archives of Canada: pages 9, 12, 15, 26 (r), 27, 28, 29, 30, 31, 33, 34, 40, 41, 42, 44, 45, 46, 51, 54, 52, 53, 55 (r), 56 (l&r), 58, 59, 62, 63, 64 (l&r), 65, 66, 68, 71, 75, 76, 77, 78 (l&r), 79, 80, 81, 63, 84, 85, 86, 88, 90, 91, 92, 93, 95, 97, 98, 100, 101, 102, 103, 108, 109, 111, 113, 114, 115, 116, 117, 118, 119, 120, 121, 123.

Photograph courtesy of Mrs. E. Virgulti: page 11.

Photograph courtesy of the Archives and Museum, The Toronto Board of Education: page 13(l).

Photograph courtesy of the City of Toronto Archives, RG 8, Parks #199: page 13(r).

Drawing courtesy of Jakubowski, *The Telegram*, November 20, 1959: page 14.

Photograph courtesy of the Archives, Ridley College: pages 17, 18, 19, 20, 21, 23.

Photograph courtesy of the Hockey Hall of Fame: page 26(l).

Photograph courtesy of *The Toronto Star*, June 30, 1928: page 35.

Photograph courtesy of *The Globe and Mail*, March 10, 1937: page 38.

Photograph courtesy of *The Toronto Star*, August 6, 1975: page 117.

Photograph courtesy of *The Evening Telegram*, February 2, 1939: page 60.

Cartoon courtesy of *The Evening Telegram*, February 7, 1931: page 37.

CFL Fact Book courtesy of the Canadian Football Hall of Fame & Museum: page 55(l)

Program courtesy of Mr. Lou MacPherson: page 44.

Photograph courtesy of The Butler Photograph Collection, Superior Public Library, Superior, Wisconsin: pages 72, 73.

Photograph courtesy of the Metropolitan Toronto Reference Library: page 38, 48, 55, 87.

Photograph courtesy of Mrs. Beverly Campbell: page 110.

ACKNOWLEDGEMENTS

I would like to acknowledge and thank the following, whose brands were mentioned in this book:

Chesebrough-Pond's Canada, Vaseline; Best Foods Canada Inc., Crown Brand Corn Syrup, Bee Hive Corn Syrup; Castrol Canada Inc., Castrol Motor Oil; Hershey Canada Inc., Lowney's "Oh Henry!"®; Cadbury Beverages Canada Inc., Canada Dry; Eveready Division, Ralston Purina Canada Inc, Eveready Batteries; Colgate Palmolive Canada Inc., Colgate Chlorophyll Toothpaste.

I have made every effort to contact those whose products were part of Harry Foster's career and are mentioned in the book.

Index